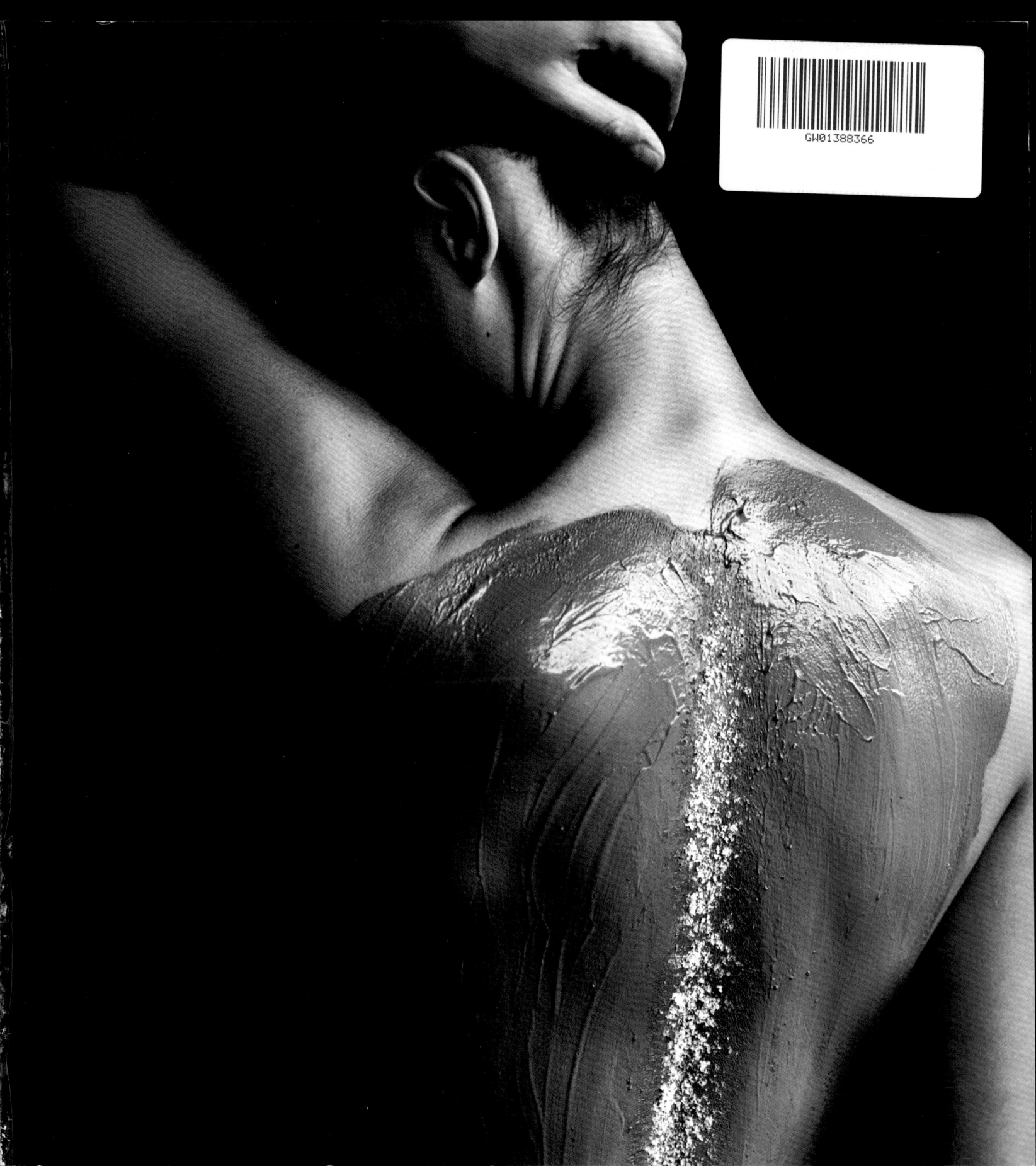

Australia's Best Spas

The Ultimate Guide to Luxury and Relaxation

by Amanda Jane Clark
Photography by Ashley Mackevicius

PERIPLUS

AUTHOR'S NOTE: Researching this book was the best job I have ever had. Months of fabulous treatments left me feeling fantastic and I apparently looked pretty radiant too. I am now completely hooked on the pure pleasure, both physical and mental, that regular spa visits bestow—not to mention the amazing health benefits. My deepest thanks to everyone who helped make this book a reality!

Published by Periplus Editions, with editorial offices at 130 Joo Seng Road #06-01, Singapore 368357.

Distributed by:
North America, Latin America and Europe
Tuttle Publishing, 364 Innovation Drive,
North Clarendon, VT 05759-9436, USA
Tel: (802) 773 8930; Fax: (802) 773 6993
Email: info@tuttlepublishing.com
www.tuttlepublishing.com

Asia Pacific Berkeley Books Pte Ltd, 130 Joo Seng Road #06-01,
Singapore 368357
Tel: (65) 6280 1330; Fax: (65) 6280 6290
Email: inquiries@periplus.com.sg
www.periplus.com

Indonesia PT Java Books Indonesia, Jl. Kelapa Gading Kirana,
Blok A14 No. 17, Jakarta 14240, Indonesia
Tel: 62 (21) 451 5351; Fax: 62 (21) 453 4987
Email: cs@javabooks.co.id

Page 1: Lilianfels Blue Mountains Resort and Spa,
New South Wales
Page 2: Crown Spa, Crown Towers, Melbourne
This page: Waldheim Spa, Cradle Mountain Lodge, Tasmania
Facing contents page: Aurora Spa Retreat, Melbourne

10 09 08 07 06 05
8 7 6 5 4 3 2 1

Contents

Health, Relaxation and Wellbeing—Australian Style

A little pampering can go a long way. Imagine lying in a fragrant rainforest spa while a gentle, warm rain drums a hypnotic rhythm over you. You roll over and someone hands you a divinely soft bath robe and delicious iced tea, which you sip while your feet and legs are massaged. That pesky ache in your shoulder has vanished after expert attention from your therapist's nimble fingers and the essential oil blend mixed especially for you has worked its heady aromatherapy magic on your mind and body. You feel deeply relaxed and blissful….

Step away from the stresses of daily living and see life from a different perspective. Exotic escapes and sublime indulgences that will leave you looking and feeling your ultimate best await you in Australia's multitude of spas.

Getting there is definitely part of the fun. Your journey to inspiring locations will take you through magnificent national parks, to sparkling oceans and sandy beaches, across breathtaking harbours, into glamorous cityscapes and remote landscapes rich in ancient wonders.

Even if it were possible to visit a different spa each month, it would take several years to experience the varied delights of every Australian spa. From just four spas in the late 1990s, there are now over 300, with a dozen more opening in 2005. The figure continues to rise, as spa visits become an essential component of many holidays and we utilise spa treatments as a method to reduce stress, feel good and live longer.

Australia is blessed with a mind-boggling array of spas in a multitude of shapes, sizes and locations. While not able to include even a quarter of the wonderful spas available in every corner of the country, this book highlights the best quality spas that await you in premier locations, from Queensland's palm fringed golden coastline to Tasmania's wild mountain wilderness. It also provides recipes to allow you to indulge in, or at least reminisce about, a few of the blissful and pampering body treatments and deliciously healthy spa cuisine you will encounter, at home.

A spa's treatment menu and design are strongly influenced by it's location—for example warming treatments and plenty of steam rooms and hot spa baths are available in cool climate locations such as Cradle Mountain in Tasmania, Lilianfels in the Blue Mountains of New South Wales and Breathtaker Retreat at Mount Buller in the Victorian Alps. Spas in warmer tropical locations specialise in developing innovative ways to keep you cool, soothe your sun-kissed skin and make it glow. There's nothing like a body polish, massage or perhaps even a spray-on tan to make you proud to show a little flesh.

OPPOSITE: The spectacularly lit, mosaic-tiled pool at the glamorous Park Club Health and Day Spa, Park Hyatt, Melbourne.

SPA GUESTS HAVE THE OPPORTUNITY TO TAKE TIME TO LISTEN TO THEIR SOULS AND THEIR BODIES
— *JANE SEGERBERG*

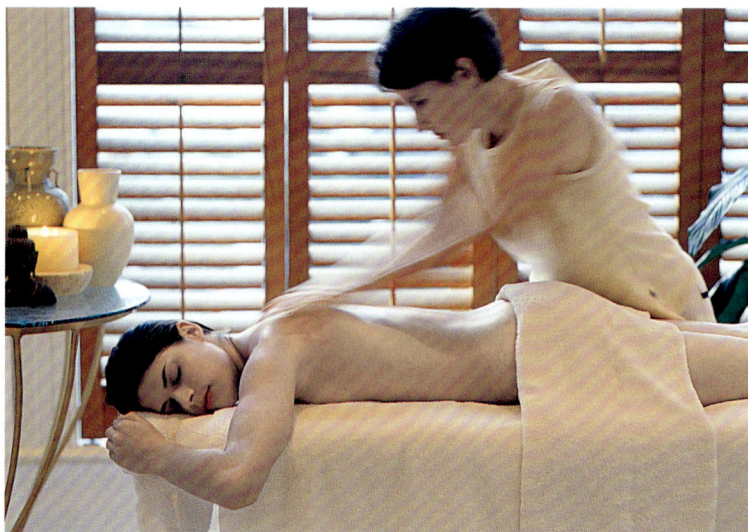

ABOVE: At The Dome Retreat in Brisbane, guests are taken to another world that is simply divine. OPPOSITE: It may be cold outside but the heated indoor pool at Lilianfels Blue Mountains Resort and Spa feels like sun-warmed rain.

In our society of abundance—peace of mind and personal time-out to relax, reflect and rejuvenate have become precious, often elusive treasures. Restorative and balancing treatments provided in a peaceful spa environment are an effective counter to the pressures of our modern lifestyle. Whether your spa visit is a treat or a regular date, for an hour, a day or a week, the combination of traditional methods with the best scientific research, latest equipment and pure natural products makes today's spa experience an indulgence that is good for you.

Apart from the obvious physical benefits, a spa visit can be a spiritually euphoric experience. With all the laying of hands, cleansing and renewal, sensory stimulation and heightened awareness of

our physical presence, the effect of submitting to treatments designed to deliver ultimate pleasure can be mind altering.

The spa experience is your time to relax, reflect, revitalise and rejoice. As international spa professional Jane Segerberg elaborates, "Spa guests have the opportunity to take time to listen to their souls and their bodies. Personal issues are resolved, new horizons are identified, a new perspective and understanding is achieved, new friendships are established, and old relationships are reconfirmed. Spas achieve these miracles in a number of ways, from relaxing treatments to mountaintop experiences, experiential walks, water therapies, clairvoyant readings, meditation, yoga, hikes, lifestyle balancing and nature."

It has become de rigueur for many holidaymakers to plan at least one spa visit during their vacation, and hotels and resorts are often chosen because of the spa facilities available. Couples are well catered for, with treatments providing an intimate opportunity to share a sublime experience so rarely available within our normal workaday routines. So popular are spa visits at many hotels and resorts that guests are advised to book their treatments before they arrive, to avoid the disappointment of finding the spa fully booked.

While a nurturing touch will always be at the heart of any great treatment, the latest spa trends include more energy healing treatments like Reiki massage, and steam facilities such as the

amazing hydrostorm—a glass cocoon for two where water jets of every strength can be angled to every part of your body while aromatic steam and coloured lights tantalise your senses. Exotic steam environments like the often beautifully decorated and domed Middle Eastern Rasul are appearing in new spas and there is an awareness of the need to use less water. To this end the hydrotherm cocoon is often chosen over the Vichy shower in areas prone to drought and water restrictions. Hot stone massage is popular and more men are requesting facials and massage as therapy versus luxury.

It seems the older the knowledge incorporated into a treatment the better, and the more esoteric the tradition, the more impressed we are with it. As Australia's spa guru Kirien Withers explains, "We are steaming in Rasuls, healing on Aboriginal healing beds, awakening our third eye with ayurvedic shirodhara and releasing under native American hot rocks. Steam, massage and water therapies, along with herbs and natural ingredients are the common threads."

Australia is the world leader in incorporating organic, pure and natural ingredients into beauty products and many spas are using outstanding Australian-made spa products such as Sodashi, Li'Tya and MV Organic Skincare. The experience of being enveloped by traditional Australian

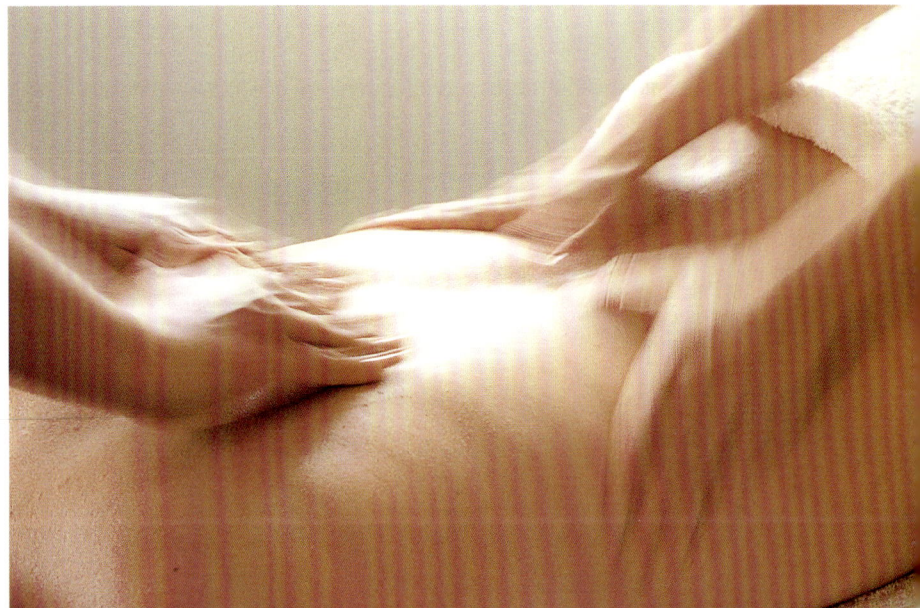

healing rituals and the ethereal power of Australian bush flower essences is amazing.

There are four major types of spas in Australia— the retreat spa, the resort spa, the day spa and the salon or mini spa. Retreat spas such as the Golden Door Health Retreats in Queensland and New South Wales are havens tucked away from the world, in the country wilds or near the ocean. Here, you can literally retreat from your daily life to focus totally on your wellbeing—to completely refresh and renew, or address particular health and lifestyle concerns. Resort spas such as the

ABOVE: Four hands are far better than two when it comes to Aurora's relaxing double massage.
OPPOSITE: Experiencing the Vichy shower in the Healing Waters Spa at Silky Oaks Lodge is the closest you may come to lying naked in a forest while being caressed by a warm gentle rain. This is truly fantasy-making stuff indeed.

SPAS WILL BE THE PERSONAL TRAINERS OF THIS NEW CENTURY
— SUZANNE DAWSON

A great spa should excite our senses and make us feel special, in both a physical and emotional way. Its luxurious pampering and healing treatments will be offered in a safe, nurturing environment and while it does not need to dazzle us with design and décor, it should be welcoming, sparkling clean, comfortable and inviting. Spas release you from the trappings of your ordinary image of yourself. A great spa will rub your mind, body and soul the right way.

The Australian spa is sophisticated yet down to earth, energised and vital, life enriching and yet still accessible. With the inspired guidance of skilled professionals and a heavenly spa environment designed to delight our senses and meet our every need, we have the blessed opportunity to experience the kind of pleasure, relaxation and renewal we may not have known existed. A sublime spa experience can unlock an energy deep within you and facilitate personal change and self-discovery. It can provide balance and unleash our body's natural ability to heal itself. A spa visit can give you the time and space to solve a previously intractable problem or soothe the effects of some of life's savagery. In this light the question becomes—can we afford not to visit a spa regularly? No wonder new spas, each individually wonderful and unique, are appearing faster than we can visit them. Happy spa-ing and remember, there will always be a new spa treatment to experience somewhere in Australia that is worth travelling to. Enjoy!

ABOVE: Indigenous ingredients and healing techniques inspired the natural spa products in the Li'Tya range.
OPPOSITE: The Vichy shower bed at Daintree Eco Lodge, carved into the shape of a leaf from the ylang ylang tree that grows in the surrounding rainforest.
PAGES 16-17: At the beach in Palm Cove outside Espa in Queensland.

Sun Spa at Hyatt Regency Coolum or The Spa and Total Living Centre at Couran Cove Resort on South Stradbroke Island are generally attached to a full resort and offer lifestyle balancing and rejuvenating treatments. Day spas are the fastest growing sector of the industry, found either within a hotel like The Spa at the Mansion Hotel in Melbourne, or standing alone in an urban environment, like the Gillian Adams Salon and Spa in Sydney. They offer a range of pampering and therapeutic treatments along with self-care and lifestyle balancing education. Salon or mini spas offer spa-style treatments and service standards, such as waxing, manicures and facials, that are within a more traditional salon environment.

Australia's
24 Best Spas

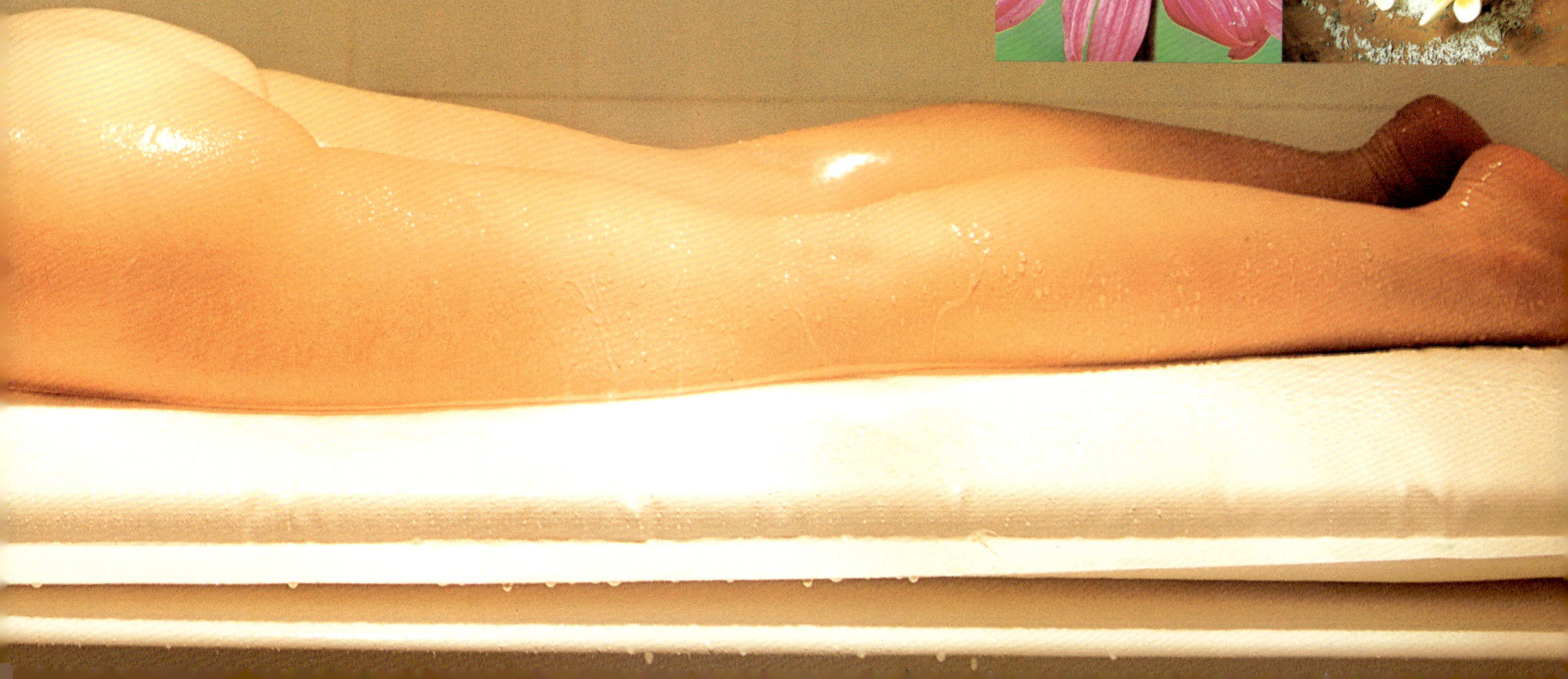

Daintree Eco Lodge and Spa, Far North Queensland

With the world's oldest living rainforest providing a dramatic and spiritually charged backdrop, complete with natural special effects such as soft, filtered daylight and pure, oxygen-rich air, your spa experience here begins long before you peruse the treatment menu.

At the heart of this environmental miracle known as the Wet Tropics World Heritage Area—where jungle clad mountains really do touch the blue coral sea—is a 12-hectare property whose spa is designed to complement activities enjoyed in the region. A massage after bushwalking, a body wrap to hydrate and soothe after a day on the reef, or a tropical rain Vichy shower on the timber wet-bed carved in the shape of an ylang ylang leaf, are offered by therapists. Although you'd be hard pressed to remain stressed for long in this soothing environment, this spa also does a lot of work in stress management.

Working closely with the local Aboriginal community, the Ku Ku Yalangi tribe, the lodge offers cultural and educational interaction through art, history, music and guided walks. Particularly special is a visit to a secluded waterfall, a sacred site where Aboriginal women were known to gather medicinal plants and bathe. Rare plants that can only survive in highly oxygenated environments thrive here. Not surprisingly, the site

ABOVE: Guest suites, resembling tree houses, are nestled within the rainforest canopy.

ABOVE AND RIGHT: With its rainforest location, the Daintree Eco Lodge and Spa promises to be the ultimate Far North Queensland restorative and indulgent experience. Exotic tropical flowers and fruit thrive in the gardens surrounding this tropical guesthouse and spa, located approximately 90 minutes' drive north of Cairns International Airport.

is said to be rich in healing energy. The signature treatment at this award-winning spa is called Walbul-Walbul, meaning "butterfly." An experience of contrasting sensations, it begins with a warm oil and desert salt exfoliation, followed by a red ochre mud wrap and Milkanga Kaday head treatment, finishing with the healing waters of the rain showers and a soothing massage to unite your spirit with the blue skies. They liken this treatment to the brilliant transition of a caterpillar into a beautiful butterfly. Silken skin, environment-induced euphoria and perhaps the whisper of an ancient mystery are also guaranteed.

The environment and its restorative qualities are the inspiration behind Daintree Eco Lodge. Exotically remote but easily accessible, this family owned and managed lodge provides 15 luxurious and private tree houses, some with balcony spa baths. The symphonic chorus of generally unseen but heard frogs, birds and insects renders pan-flute CDs redundant. The rain, the forest and its everyday natural life were the inspiration for the spa's design, and water, which flows from the waterfall to the lodge and spa, is harnessed for drinking and for spa treatments.

To complement the spa experience, classes are offered in Ki meditation and yoga. Ki is derived from the principles of Japanese Aikido. It focuses on achieving harmony and direct physical energy with the mind, through a combination of basic breathing exercises, correct posture, true relaxation and meditation. Casual visitors and guests alike are invited to try it out.

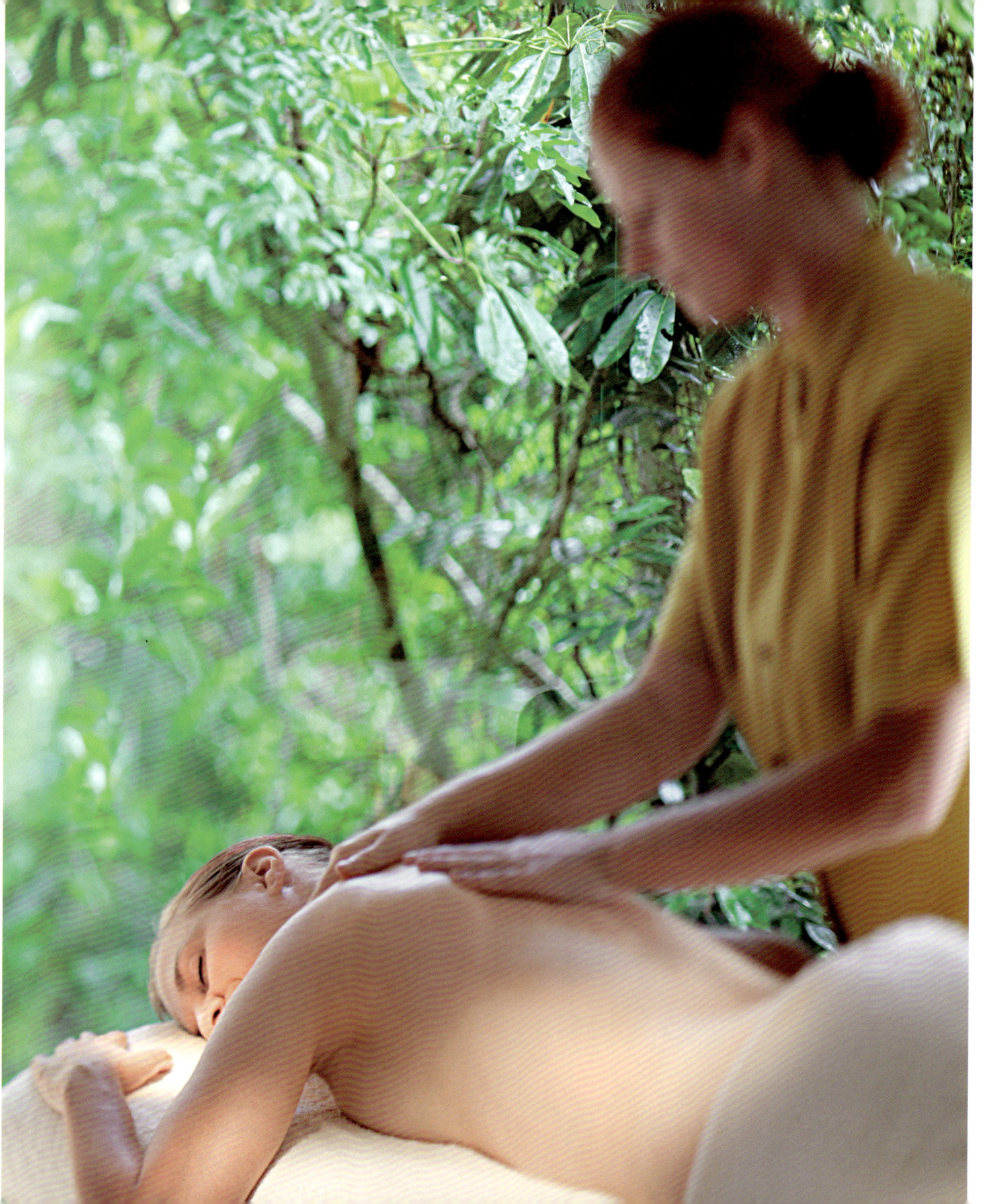

Healing Waters Spa, Silky Oaks Lodge, Far North Queensland

Cocooned within the vibrant, lush Daintree Rainforest, a landscape that resonates with ancient ceremonies and whispers of sacred healings, this spa takes the concept of "communing with nature" to a special level.

The spiritually-charged energies of the rainforest were revered by the Aborigines of the Mossman Gorge region, who gathered medicinal plants here and bathed in the river which flows below Silky Oaks Lodge. Inspired by traditional, indigenous wisdom and the life-renewing qualities of the Mossman River, known as "the Healing Waters" by local Aboriginal people, an aura of abundance, serenity and fertility permeates this spa.

Nesting in the treetops above the river and connected by a maze of boardwalks and pathways through the enveloping vegetation, the magical beauty and natural wonders surrounding the tree house guest suites and spa hardly seem real, more like the creation of special effects artists.

Healing Waters Spa is located an hour north of Cairns in a timber pavilion at the end of a fragrant pathway. The primary architect here is nature, brilliantly enhanced by a stunningly designed space through which guests and staff flow as naturally as a gentle breeze through the rainforest. Vast walls of glass fill every room with fresh air and natural light, filtered through a geometric tapestry of palms, ferns and flowers. The earthy tones of natural wood, stone floors and chocolate or magenta-coloured lounges, contrasts stunningly with the myriad shades of green foliage, visible at every turn. In a spacious, slate-floored couples suite, an over-sized shower rose cascades water from the ceiling into a sunken bath, just a few feet from the rainforest. For guest's aural pleasure, a well amplified, natural symphony is kindly provided by thousands of insects, birds, animals and rustling leaves.

Treatments using Li'Tya products, based on native berries, herbs and plants, draw on the knowledge of

OPPOSITE: A soothing massage in a tropical rainforest is pure bliss.

BELOW: Australian spa products good enough to eat are used here.

Aboriginal people to nurture and heal, while treatments using Sodashi products, based on aromatic plant essences, focus on achieving a holistic wellness. Naturally, all treatments have been designed to bestow pleasure and relaxation, while leaving your skin feeling enriched, energised and glowing with health.

Simple touches add to the delights provided here, from fresh iced teas to the energy cleansing quartz crystals and miniature wooden coolamons (a basin-shaped dish traditionally made and used by Aborigines) adorning each treatment table. The tropical atmosphere is relaxed, warm and open, while the environment is exotic and exciting. It's the kind of place you will love to revisit and remember when you need a little escape from reality— I'm back there right now.

ABOVE: The surrounding forest and light are almost a design element in this spa, ensuring that all who enter are soaked in nature's healing calm.

RIGHT: Guests are pampered with Vichy showers, de-stressing baths, facials and detox treatments, using all-natural products from the all-Australian brands Li'Tya and Sodashi.

Espa, The Reef House, Palm Cove, Queensland

Discreetly obscured by abundant tropical gardens and gigantic melaleuca gums, the seaside village of Palm Cove in North Queensland emanates a relaxed yet sophisticated ambience. It's as if everyone feels slightly smug about their good fortune to be here. Only a 30-minute drive north of Cairns, Palm Cove is the domain of a growing number of hotel and resort spas, each nurturing an individual character and offering exquisite experiences in beauty, health and wellbeing. With a handful of glamorous spas scattered along the beachfront, the locally bestowed title of "Spa Capital of Australia" fits well.

Thanks to some thoughtful planning, no building here is taller than the coconut palms lining the long, white sandy beach. This ensures that the soul-inspiring view you'll discover from the jetty opposite Espa, is of rainforest-covered mountains sweeping down to meet the sparkling aqua of the Coral Sea.

Framed by fuchsia, origami-like flowers of bougainvillea vines and fragrant frangipani trees, Espa's home is a whitewashed, timber-shuttered building beside a cascading waterfall in the grounds of the Reef House Hotel. Once the home of a brigadier, the hotel's design and service, along with touches such as candlelit corridors and an honour bar adorned with primitive art, reflect the romance of a bygone era.

The casual elegance of the languidly exotic spa could be described as "plantation style meets shabby chic."

THIS PAGE AND OPPOSITE: Surrounded by tropical blooms, verdant foliage and gentle waterfalls, Espa is the perfect Eden where many a tired soul finds rest and healing.

LEFT AND RIGHT: Enriched by 10 years' experience in creating upmarket spas worldwide, the Espa team now offers design consultancy services that aim at enhancing the environment as part of the total spa experience.

Terracotta-tiled floors, carved wooden candle mounts, white timber furniture and the spicy aroma of Espa's tropical blend of essential oils permeate the five spacious treatment rooms and relaxation areas.

Espa features Li'Tya spa products, which integrate precious qualities of the Australian earth with its native plants and spirit. Treatments offered combine the wisdom of Aboriginal spirituality and healing methods with aromatherapy and herbalist principles to produce powerful experiences for body and soul. Espa's signature treatment, the Mala Mayi (clan food— Arnhem Land) is a luscious full body, rejuvenation affair. An individually designed treatment, guests choose between reharmonising, rejuvenating or detoxifying blends of clay, salt and oil, which are then used to cleanse, exfoliate, massage and energise.

Treatments begin with a soothing footbath and the indigenous ritual of "smudging," where bark and flowers are burnt (the effect is like incense) to cleanse a space of negative energies and centre a person's spirit into the room. Espa's nurturing and generous ambience is obvious in the little things, like a pot of fresh tea and an invitation to relax in a peaceful lounge area, post pampering. It all contributes to a deeply satisfying spa experience.

In January 2004, Espa was recognised as one of the "Best 100 Spas of the World" by *Harpers and Queens* London.

The Spa of Peace and Plenty, Dunk Island, Queensland

Beyond the coconut palms that fringe this lush tropical island, hidden within a tranquil rainforest garden, an airy, Balinese-style timber pavilion is waiting to warmly welcome you. A footbridge leads the way to the doors of this Paradise, which is also the place to leave your cares and allow your senses free rein.

A nurturing energy infuses every aspect of this thoughtfully operated spa, thanks to a caring, professional staff. While your feet are gently washed, sit back with a glass of fresh strawberry, lime and orange-infused water and drink in the tranquility. The spa's unique signature scent, an exotic combination of lime, blood orange patchouli, rose, ylang ylang jasmine and geranium fills the air, leading your senses on an enriching journey of renewal.

Dunk Island can be reached by light aircraft (45 minutes) or coach and launch (2 hours) from Cairns International Airport. The original inhabitants of Dunk Island, the Djiru Aboriginal tribe, named it Coonanglebah—the

isle of peace and plenty, a moniker that still fits. The fertile environment provides the fruit and flowers found in the spa while the ocean's presence is reflected in many of the delights on the spa menu. An inspired range of treatments specially designed

for the tropics is available, including the Mermaid's Song, an exotic body polish which leaves your skin softened to perfection. A crushed pearl peel is first used to polish the body before it is deeply relaxed in an oil and Dead Sea salt-infused bath. A fragrant

OPPOSITE: The Ayurvedic treatment Shirodhara can induce a calm, blissful state of serenity and expanded relaxation.

ABOVE: This spa's modern and organic design features many spaces dedicated to reflection and relaxation.

LEFT AND OPPOSITE: Stone, wood, leaf, flower, water—The Spa of Peace and Plenty knows that the best things in life are the simple ones. Flowers and herbs used in treatments are grown on the island. Relax with someone you love.

toning mist is then applied to the body and a moisturising milk massaged into the skin, giving it a radiant glow. The treats continue afterwards, with a refreshing sorbet served in the meditation lounge to all guests, who are then invited to linger longer in one of the many inviting relaxation nooks.

This spa was founded on the philosophy of helping people feel fabulous, wherever they are in their lives. As the original spa director, Luisa Anderson, said, "Our treatments are wonderful to give, magical to receive and deeply healing. We also hope they provide an exquisite transforming experience."

Much about Dunk Island complements the post-spa state of mind, which in my experience meant being so relaxed I could barely walk or talk. Fortunately there are plenty of divine spots to do nothing more than contemplate the view in bliss and oblivion, while someone brings you delicious things to nibble and sip. This is the perfect place to enjoy a generous slice of spa lifestyle.

The Sun Spa, Hyatt Regency Coolum, Queensland

Designed as a luxury destination spa in the late 1980s, this grand dame of Australian resort spas continues to lead the way into unchartered spa territory. Recent expansion has created a visually thrilling spa filled with many unusual features, such as colour therapy lights which change the colour of a room.

Located about ninety minutes north of Brisbane Airport and only half an hour from the trendy resort town of Noosa, the Sun Spa has 19 treatment rooms and optional spa suites (booking one is a must). A place of sun-dappled walls and glowing skylights, spa suites feature baths in secluded courtyards over-looked by native trees, while the sight and sound of falling water is ever present.

Set in 150 hectares of Queensland rainforest and bushland and facing miles of deserted ocean beach, this picturesque resort is lauded for its great service, excellent conference facilities and fantastic childcare options. The Sun Spa's "adults only" facilities, spread over 8,000 square metres, include a 25-metre heated outdoor lap pool, aquasize pool, gymnasium, aerobics and yoga studio, squash courts and hair and beauty salon. The resort also has an 18-hole golf course, tennis courts, bicycles, bushwalking tracks and nine swimming pools.

Treatments are naturally inspired by the sun. Essential oils used during body treatments and massages combine with the sun's daily phases, for example the invigorating Sun Rise blend combines lemon, grapefruit, orange, lime and basil oils, while Sun Day is a reflective blend of eucalyptus, lavender, niaouli, tea tree and peppermint.

Sun Spa lifestyle services include personal training, fitness checks, swimming or golf lessons and daily physical classes such as aerobics, yoga, belly dancing or tai chi.

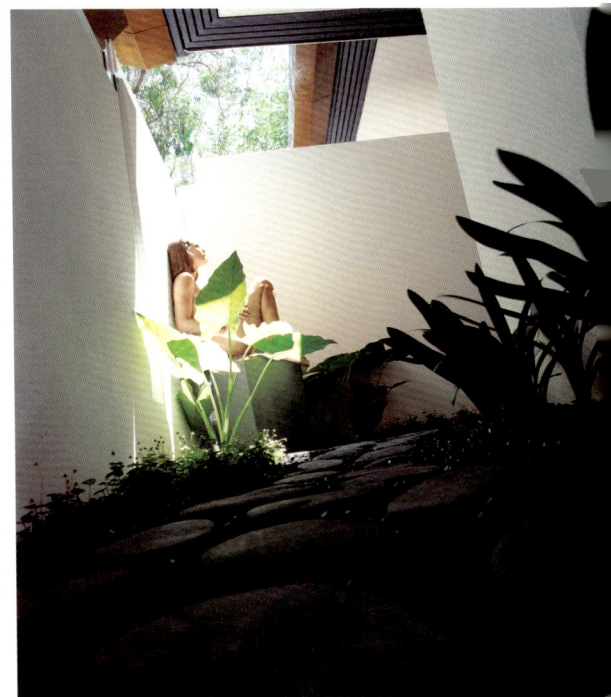

ABOVE AND LEFT: Laid-back, kid-friendly and with the Queensland sun overhead, the Hyatt Regency Coolum has something to offer guests big and small.

The Spa and Total Living Centre, Couran Cove Resort, South Stradbroke Island, Queensland

Couran Cove is a resort for the new century: an unspoiled, environmentally sensitive five-star luxury retreat without the stuffiness. A short boat ride away from Queensland's Gold Coast, Couran Cove has established itself on an island that has every type of Australian bushland (except desert) represented within its boundaries.

The resort combines wonderful natural playgrounds, like 20 kilometres of shell-covered surf beach, mature native bushland and tropical rainforest, with activities from rock-climbing to hydrocycling to Olympic-standard athletic facilities.

The Spa building is recognisably Queensland, incorporating corrugated iron, timber, batten sunshades and painted weatherboard. Inside, fresh air and natural light predominate. The high-angled ceilings, large sun decks, polished floorboards and plantation louvre panels contribute to the beach holiday atmosphere. As part of the island's Total Living Centre, the aim of which is to help you "live better longer," the spa offers treatments and massages, naturopathic and lifestyle consultations, yoga and tai chi classes and three- or five-day resident lifestyle programmes.

A blissful hydrotherapy treatment can be experienced in the open, tiled flotation pool. Another spa specialty is a full body exfoliation and massage in the steam room, followed by a detoxifying thalassotherapy treatment in the hydrotherapy bath. Two waterside massage huts opposite the main spa have floor-to-ceiling blinds that open, so it seems there is nothing between you and nature.

The resort's founder, the former Australian Olympian Ron Clarke, has succeeded in his aim of bringing people and nature together in a relaxed family environment. The extent to which the resort goes in its commitment to adopt the motto "as nature would have it" is astounding, and includes worm farms, solar power and televisions that tell you how much energy your unit has used.

Pedal or foot power is the best way to explore Couran Cove's 161 hectares and to enjoy the huge range of sporting and leisure activities. Participate in as much or as little as you choose and when the day is done, a selection of restaurants offer delicious spa cuisine or other higher-calorie options. The choice is yours. Relax and enjoy.

LEFT AND RIGHT: Suspended above a tidal lagoon, close to the resort's harbourside epicentre, the well-equipped spa is modern and smart in design and operation.

THE DOME RETREAT'S PHILOSOPHY IS BASED ON AYURVEDA, AN ANCIENT METHOD OF HEALING PRACTISED THROUGHOUT INDIA FOR THOUSANDS OF YEARS

The Dome Retreat, Marriott Hotel, Brisbane

A gentle atmosphere welcomes guests as they open the front door of this inner-city sanctuary. Peaceful music, hushed voices and calm staff in earth-coloured, natural-fibre uniforms can have the worries of the world slipping from your shoulders faster than you can say "replenish me."

The spa's creator, Meaghan South, wanted to provide a place where people could "escape for a day that's pure" and leave feeling rejuvenated, revitalised and renewed. The Dome Retreat's philosophy is based on Ayurveda, an ancient method of healing practised throughout India for thousands of years. Emphasizing preventative and healing therapies, along with various methods of purification and rejuvenation, Ayurvedic treatments aim to balance, harmonise and nurture the body and soul.

Attentive, individual nurturing and pampering is high on the agenda at The Dome Retreat and the experienced therapists are aware of the importance of touch and the fact that many people don't get enough of it.

Frangipani, other tropical blooms and Southeast Asian furniture are hallmarks of this spa. Six attractive and well-equipped treatment or massage rooms and two wet rooms are decorated with an eclectic mix of Buddhist relics and Indian artefacts collected by Meaghan on her travels.

Situated on the fourth floor of the five-star Marriott Hotel, The Dome Retreat's relaxation lounge and balcony overlooks the Brisbane River. Weather permitting, tall wooden doors are thrown open, allowing sunshine and fresh air to warm your toes and fill your lungs as you relax on the comfy cane lounges sipping herbal tea.

The nourishing organic products used are made from essential flower and plant essences and bestow the potent benefits of aromatherapy.

Besides offering a wide range of face and body treatments, hydrotherapy baths, Vichy showers and massages, The Dome Retreat encourages and supports clients to achieve health and wellbeing goals. Naturopath and lifestyle consultations, coaching or fitness assessments, yoga, macro-biotic and astrological guidance can be arranged.

LEFT: Guests are encouraged to linger at the Retreat before and after treatments. The hotel sauna and pool are open to spa visitors and there are many pleasant settings for a healthy spa cuisine lunch.

Paradise Spa and Bath House, Surfers Paradise, Queensland

Queensland's Gold Coast is home to many exciting theme park worlds— Sea World, Movie World and now a spa which could become known as Spa World. A true spa in that a dazzling variety of water therapies are available, Paradise Spa is also fun, in a great Surfers Paradise kind of way. You can even leave with a spray-on tan and blow-dry to rival any local.

Located in downtown Surfers Paradise, one of the first things you notice is the dramatic lighting. Opulent purple surfaces reflect a slowly changing, rainbow-coloured glow, the light and colour contributing to the celebratory atmosphere of this below-ground spa.

Treatments offered in the eleven culturally themed therapy rooms touch on a combination of exotic cultures and include Thai massage, Hawaiian Lomi-Lomi, Chinese Tui-Na, Indian Ayurvedic, Japanese Shiatsu, reflexology and Middle Eastern massage. It's no surprise that the menu also offers an eight-hour treatment of ultimate indulgence called "Around the world in a day."

Guests begin their journey through Paradise with a brief full body exfoliation. This prepares the skin to reap the benefits of the hydrotherapy treatments. Within a spacious unisex area the hot ginseng pool bestows a revitalizing and regulating effect, while the non-chlorinated (ozone) "spirit" pool contains 400 strategically placed water massage jets and several submerged "spa lounges."

Male and female domains each have a sauna, hot salt bath, cold plunge pool, steam and exfoliation rooms and a mosaic-tiled Rasul steam temple where guests are exfoliated with a cinnamon-vanilla body scrub and painted with a chakra mud while inhaling herb-infused steam. A cleansing warm rain which falls from the starlit ceiling completes this heavenly experience. This spa may be quirky, but it was impossible to wipe the smile off my face in this little piece of paradise.

BELOW: Water therapies are an integral component of this spa. OPPOSITE: The decor is colourful and upbeat and the therapists are hand picked for their skill and experience.

Azabu, Byron Bay, New South Wales

The ancient forest of native hoop pines and rainforest surrounding the Azabu guesthouse and spa contributes to this property's serene and spiritual atmosphere. Towering over the five interconnected suites like the steeple of a cathedral, the trees provide an aromatic backdrop for restful contemplation. Positioned in the foothills behind Byron Bay on the north coast of New South Wales, where alternative lifestyles are considered mainstream, Azabu is a boutique luxury retreat with a lot of style. Azabu's hosts believe people today want and need more bliss in their lives and will do their best to provide it. Space, time and privacy work together here to soothe and relax guests.

The guest suites feature polished timber floors and a wall of wooden shuttered windows that fold back to invite the outside forest in. Sunken spa baths jut into the trees to emulate outdoor bathing and a lagoon-like, heated swimming pool and jacuzzi further encourage guests to release themselves to the sensual pleasures of water.

Elevated walkways lead to the spa treatment room and entertainment areas where the furnishings and décor are in an exotic, Asian style. The central building's curved walls in mulberry and earth impart an organic aura, and look as if they might uncurl and slide off into the forest. The loud, rhythmic croak of resident frogs is somnolent, and if there were really such a thing as fairies at the end of the garden you would probably find them here.

Open to visitors and houseguests, Azabu's day spa offers a balanced

ABOVE: Azabu's heated pool is like a secluded forest swimming hole.
LEFT: The guest suites at Azabu open into peaceful wilderness.
OPPOSITE: Nature is ever present in Azabu's treatment rooms.

menu of face and body treatments, massages and treatment packages. Products using plant and flower essences are based on ancient techniques of skincare combined with modern technology.

Nature is ever present in the treatment room, seen through a glass wall facing the trees, and contributes to the room's peaceful ambience.

An aura of healing energy pervades this spiritually charged region, where Aboriginal elders once gathered regularly. Legend has it that the area around Byron Bay was too sacred a place for indigenous tribes to live permanently; instead the tribes considered it an important ceremonial site and meeting place. A natural habitat for vast tea tree forests, the brown waters of tea tree infused lagoons are now used for therapeutic bathing by the locals. Whale-watching, bush-walking and surfing in the national parks and sun-worshipping at Australia's most easterly point are other attractions this area offers. The closest airports to Byron Bay are Ballina Airport (30 minutes' drive) and Coolangatta Airport (55 minutes' drive). Shuttle buses and coaches are available.

OPPOSITE AND THIS PAGE: The many facets of spa life in this spiritually charged region, known for its vast tracts of tea tree forests.

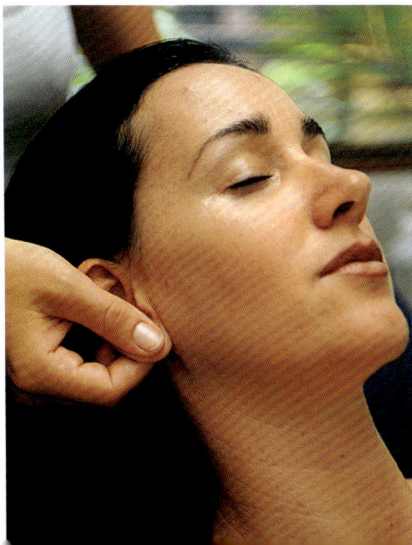

ELYSIA IS A CHRYSALIS LIKE NO OTHER, A SECLUDED PARADISE OF OPULENT LUXURY, NURTURING GUIDANCE, MOUTH-WATERING MEALS AND SENSATIONAL SPA TREATMENTS

The Golden Door Health Retreat—Elysia, Hunter Valley, New South Wales

The Golden Door Health Retreat—Elysia is something of a butterfly maker —no one leaves unchanged by their experiences here. Whether your wings have fallen off, no longer fit or are in need of a good spring-clean, Elysia is a chrysalis like no other, a secluded paradise of opulent luxury, nurturing guidance, mouth-watering meals and sensational spa treatments.

Surrounded by picturesque vineyards, patchwork valleys and distant mountain ranges, Elysia is like a modern citadel perched high above the marauding temptations and bad habits of the "real world." Totally stylish, hip and pleasing in every way, from the architecture and interior design to the investment art collection, cloud-like beds and sparkling gym, Elysia exudes good vibrations and elicits an "isn't this great and aren't we lucky to be here" energy from guests.

Concentric spiral walkways lead through a sea of lavender to the retreat's highest point, the Meditation Hill. From here, a fountain of water begins its journey through the many synergistic parts of Elysia, passing through the spa buildings, gardens and central lodge, threading them together with a life-giving force. Simultaneously soothing and invigorating, this symbolic river of life dances swiftly over river boulders in

THIS PAGE AND LEFT: With 26 dry and wet treatment rooms, wellness centre and indoor pool, you're sure to leave the spa a stronger, fitter and energised person. At Elysia, guests will discover what it feels like to experience wellness, balance and vitality.

some places and is smooth flowing and quiet in others, all the while renewing, reviving and cleansing.

The first world-class, purpose-built health retreat in Australia and the latest property in the expanding Golden Door Spa and Health Retreat group, Elysia is committed to reshaping our definition of good health. The team achieves this by enabling guests to discover what it feels like to experience wellness, balance and vitality. It's all a matter of choosing and learning the right exercise, nutrition, stress manage-ment and relaxation. The beauty of Elysia is that you don't have to worry about a thing. Elysia's comprehensive assortment of professional practitioners excel at making anything you've previously found difficult to do—be it giving

up smoking or losing weight—easy, manageable and very enjoyable.

Elysia's spa is a sanctuary of pleasure. The largest of its kind in Australia, the spa features 26 wet and dry rooms, with many unique treatments offered. One of these is the Watsu, a form of aquatic body-work with origins in Zen Shiatsu. A gentle treatment bestowing a delight-ful sensation of total weightlessness and seaweed-like flexibility, the Watsu can assist with chronic and acute pain, balance body energies, increase circulation and create a deep sense of relaxation through its gliding and flowing movements.

A multitude of activities and equip-ment are available to guests, including a 25-metre indoor lap pool, pilates studio, tennis courts, mountain bikes and wellness centre, educational

seminars, cooking classes, yoga and tai chi. Guests can choose between an independent stay (minimum two days) or the well-known Golden Door programme. The programme is available as a five- or seven-day option and has more guidance and structure than an independent stay.

All packages include accommodation, gourmet spa cuisine, full use of all facilities, a diverse range of fitness, health, education and relaxation activities, health assessment and spa treatments.

At Elysia you will be given everything you need to relax, unwind, renew, restore, invigorate, energise, enhance, explore, replenish, refresh and heal—everything you need to emerge from this special place, leaner, fitter and ready to conquer the world.

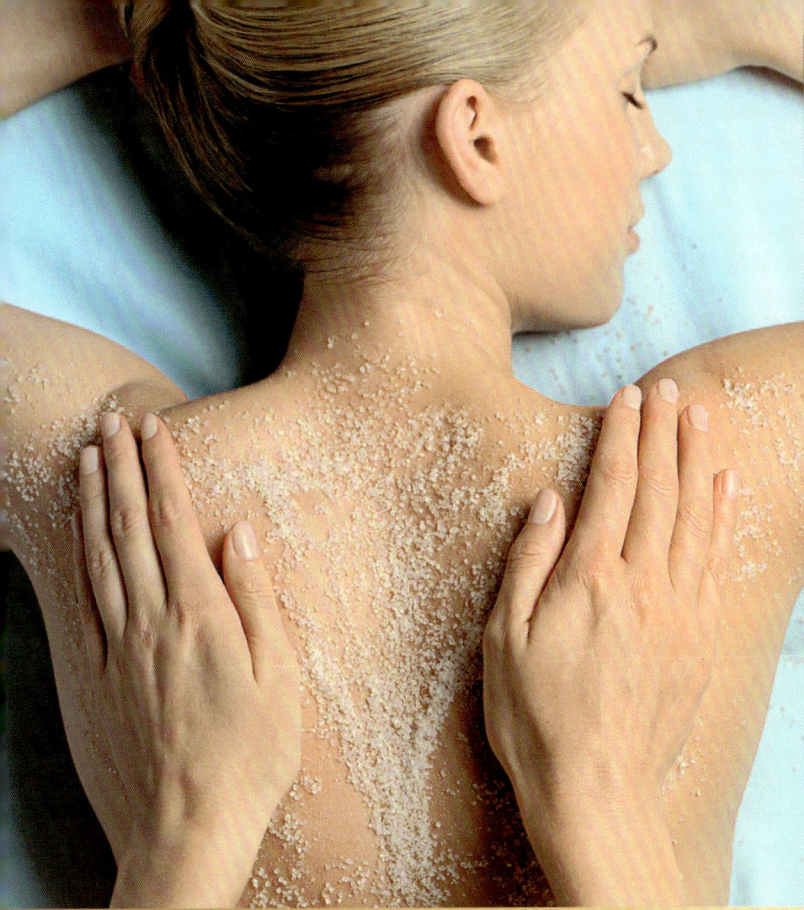

Spa Chakra, Woolloomooloo, Sydney

Sleek, chic and fashionable, Spa Chakra offers five-star delivery of over 60 treatments to balance and nurture yourself in a spectacular waterfront location. As you pull up outside the groovy W Hotel at the wharf in the Sydney city suburb of Woolloomooloo, an Armani-clad attendant greets you and valet parks your car. Along with a foot bath for new clients and a 15-minute consultation with a naturopath, these complimentary extras reflect Spa Chakra's dedication to ensuring your visit is stress-free and memorable.

Spa Chakra's modern interiors, minimalist style and illuminated marble and glass surfaces create a stylish, serene atmosphere. In this elegant world of relaxation and beauty, any or every part of the body can be renewed.

As their name suggests, Spa Chakra subscribes to the *chakra* belief system: in order to be "well" and "whole," a person must address all aspects of their body holistically— mentally, physically and spiritually.

ABOVE: Sydney's beautiful harbour and trendy Woolloomooloo wharf area is a stunning backdrop to the spa. LEFT: A detailed health questionnaire helps therapists design a treatment best suited to your needs and provides practical advice for achieving and maintaining great health and fitness.

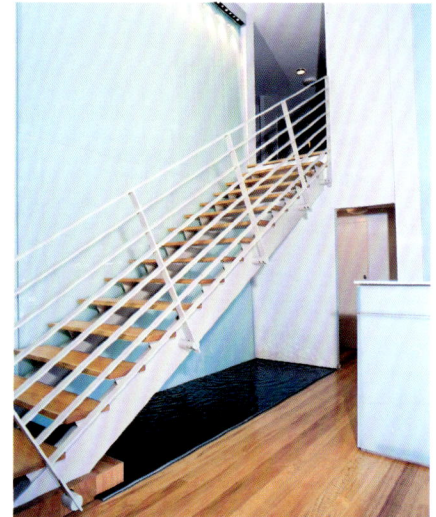

ABOVE AND LEFT: Spa Chakra's elegant world of relaxation and beauty aims to help you rediscover balance and wellbeing.

Chakras are referred to in many of the world's oldest healthcare practices and religions, and are believed to be the seven spinning wheels of energy and light aligned along a person's spine. Each *chakra* corresponds to certain components of a person's physical, emotional and spiritual being. Spa Chakra believes that almost all physical ailments have some connection to emotional, mental or spiritual issues, and have designed a range of treatments with this philosophy in mind.

Australia's only medi-spa, Spa Chakra provides comprehensive medical and wellness care in an environment that integrates spa services with conventional and complementary therapies and treatments. There are twelve treatment rooms for massage, beauty, water treatments and health practitioner consultants and two large private function rooms for special events. Tailor-made programmes can be designed for large or small groups and health retreats for three, five or seven days are also available.

A short walk from the NSW Art Gallery, Botanic Gardens, Opera House and Sydney's Central Business District, Spa Chakra and the W Hotel's waterfront location are also perfect for sightseeing, shopping and dining.

The Spa and Fitness Centre, Four Seasons Hotel, Sydney

Stress is costing the business community billions of dollars in skills loss and replacement each year as people succumb to the physical and mental effects of stress-related illness. Consequently, the corporate market is having a dramatic effect on the spread of spas. City spas in Australia report an increase in executives booking regular massages, companies bulk-buying spa gift certificates and conference organisers who prefer to book venues with spa facilities.

Located in the heart of Sydney's central business district and a short stroll from many of Sydney's major tourist attractions like the Art Gallery, Opera House and historic Rocks area, this spa is popular with locals and visitors alike. The thoughtful ability to balance the needs of busy executives and holidaymakers is evident on the spa menu where packages like The Executive Express and The Stress Buster are found alongside Seduction of the Senses and Island Indulgence.

Moss-green marble and slate, cedar, polished chrome and frosted glass are used throughout. Eight treatment rooms double as massage or wet rooms and the largest contains a double jacuzzi, combined steam and shower room and twin treatment tables. Comfortable changing rooms are fitted with a "suit mate" that dries swimsuits in five seconds.

Besides hotel guests, the spa is open to casual visitors. A range of 15- and 30-minute express treatments, like the de-stress scalp massage, express facial or neck and shoulder massage, are perfect for those in need of time out. Clients are encouraged to fully utilise the steam rooms and saunas.

The signature treatment here is very special. The intoxicating journey through the four seasons begins with brushing the body with tea tree oil to prepare the skin for further delights. Warm oil is drizzled, then massaged over the back using the nurturing Hawaiian Wave technique from toe to fingertips, followed by Reiki Chakra balancing and penetrating hot stone massage for deep relaxation. A potent Japanese silk protein treatment is then applied to the face, promising total renewal, and rejuvenation is completed with an arm and hand massage and mask.

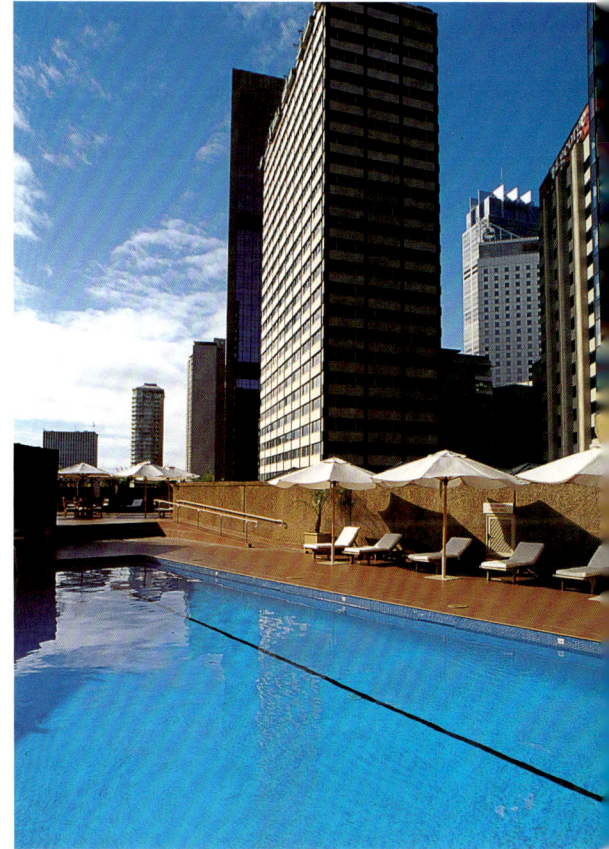

ABOVE AND FACING PAGE: The Four Seasons' Spa offers a sanctuary in the city, where an ambience of solitude and peace allow the outside world to recede from sight and mind.

Gillian Adams Salon and Spa, Turramurra, Sydney

I hope heaven is like this. If it isn't, we are fortunate that an angel named Gillian Adams has created a heavenly sanctuary for mere mortals. As the creator herself puts it, "A visit to Gillian Adams Salon and Spa should be an experience in touch and emotional healing that no one in this lifetime should neglect."

After years of research, analysis and thoughtful planning, Gillian's vision to create a truly therapeutic five-star environment embracing body, beauty, hair and wellness under one roof is a wonderful reality. A luxurious and nurturing urban haven where guests are treated to exquisite delights for body and soul, delivered with attention to detail and exceptional service.

Located 30 minutes from Sydney's CBD on the upper North Shore, it is not uncommon for guests to arrive in the spa's chauffeur-driven limousine. Chic and elegant, this glamorous spa and its devoted team of warm, caring staff made me feel like a movie star before I'd even got past the chaise lounge in the marble foyer.

The heritage-listed, Art Deco building that houses this heaven-on-earth was once a bank. Meticulously restored to its yesteryear splendour by expert craftspeople, features include hand-made curved walls and doors in American walnut and ebony timber and diffused hidden lighting throughout the cocoon-like therapy rooms.

The grand centrepiece is an AquaMedic ozone pool and steam room, as beautiful as it is therapeutic. Made entirely of crema delicata Italian marble and encased within a spectacular glass and marble chamber with a curved coffer ceiling, the water in this heated, 10-metre, chemical-free pool is as soft and pure as rainwater. A hydrotherapy playground with five separate features designed to revitalize, soothe, heal and delight, the pool's oxygen water therapy also strengthens the immune system and contributes to overall wellness, or in this case, bliss.

Beyond the many therapy rooms, a spacious relaxation lounge provides comfort, sustenance (a constantly replenished fruit platter) and views into the landscaped gardens. The chef prepares a daily spa menu, available to staff and guests. If the weather is good, lunch is served with a glass of wine beside the water sculpture in

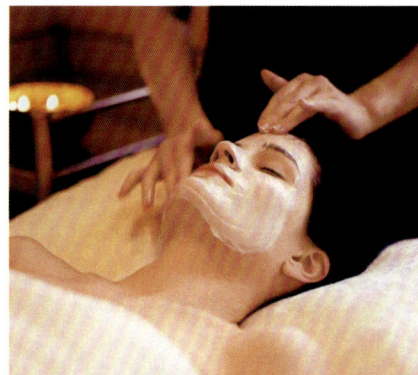

ABOVE: As befitting the aura of movie-star luxury that envelops the spa, guests receive the royal treatment and the ultimate in pampering.

RIGHT: Strong jets in the AquaMedic ozone pool give a good workout, whereas more gentle jets soothe and massage.

Gillian's very own Garden of Eden. Throughout the spa, dynamic bronze and marble sculptures by artist Helen Leete celebrate the female form and echo the feminine curves incorporated into the spa's design.

While all the big things are perfect, the little things are important here too. Most spa packages include a shampoo and blow-dry, the robes are silk, the therapists look great and even the fluffy white towels are imbued with the delectable aroma of indulgence. Now, where did I leave my wings?

THE BLUE HAZE WHICH GIVES THE MOUNTAINS THEIR NAME IS THE RESULT OF A FINE MIST OF OIL PRODUCED BY MILLIONS OF EUCALYPTUS TREES

Lilianfels Blue Mountains Resort and Spa, Blue Mountains, New South Wales

A peaceful retreat from city life on Sydney's back doorstep, the Blue Mountains have long been a popular destination for those seeking a cooler climate, clean air and the magnificent scenery and recreation offered by several large national parks in the area. The blue haze that gives the mountains their name is the result of a fine mist of oil produced by millions of eucalyptus trees, so just getting to this guesthouse spa may be counted a therapeutic experience in itself.

Despite its popularity, most of the area is so precipitous or protected that it has been impossible to over develop. Many grand country homes and their romantic English-style gardens have survived, one of which is Lilianfels. Built over one hundred years ago, when Sydneysiders first discovered the "reinvigoration of mountain air and the refined pleasure offered by the contemplation of beautiful scenery," Lilianfels occupies a spectacular, clifftop position with majestic views of mountain valleys and gorges as far as the eye can see. A much larger country house now adjoins the original Lilianfels and in keeping with its healthy roots and the restorative nature of its surroundings, it includes a spa and health club.

The atmosphere is cosy and relaxed, the service and staff attentive and friendly. Following recent and extensive renovations, the spa now has four treatment rooms, including two with baths and two for facials and

BELOW: The original guesthouse at Lilianfels now houses the retreat's five-star restaurant. OPPOSITE: Combine the spa's vast selection of top-to-toe treatments and the restorative Blue Mountain air—what else do you need to relax?

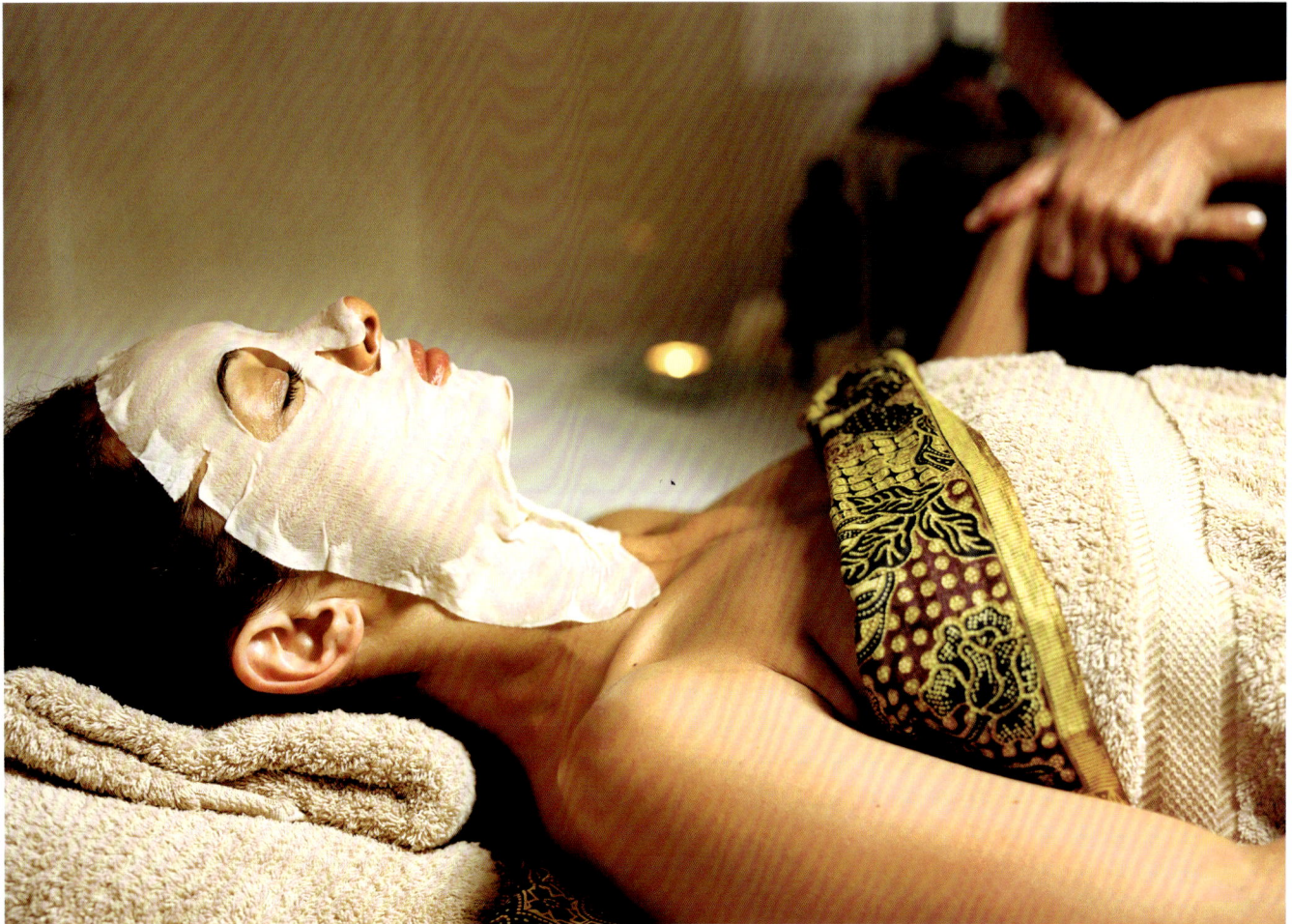

body therapy. There is a gymnasium, separate men and women's sauna, steam rooms and spa baths, and a refurbished 20-metre indoor heated pool. Guests can also lounge by an outdoor heated pool overlooking the stunning Jamison Valley. Fresh flowers, the latest magazines, candles, essential oil burners and herbal teas are comforting touches that add to the homely atmosphere.

A long, deep porcelain bath surrounded by marble was brought from the original Lilianfels House during restorations. Between treatments or on its own, a leisurely, essential oil-enhanced, candlelit soak as you sip a fresh herbal infusion of your choice is a heavenly way to spend a misty mountain afternoon.

The spa's vast selection of top-to-toe treatments combined with the restorative air of the Blue Mountains and abundance of outdoor activities including horseriding, abseiling, aqua-

OPPOSITE AND THIS PAGE: The spa uses products from the Li'Tya range in their nourishing and cleansing treatments. An inviting spa bath, sauna and steam room are added attractions in the spacious men and women's changing suites at the spa.

aerobic classes, bushwalking, tennis and golf makes this award-winning resort a perfect escape for mind, body and soul.

Salus Spa at the Lake House, Daylesford, Victoria

There is now another reason to visit the much loved and acclaimed Lake House Restaurant and Small Luxury Hotel—they have opened a day spa, called Salus. "Salus per aqum" translates from Latin to "health through water" and this spa sure knows about water. Here the ritual of bathing and taking to the waters can be enjoyed at many levels.

Ever since the original Hepburn Spa opened in 1895, people have flocked to the twin towns of Daylesford and Hepburn to experience the healing, nurturing powers of the local water. An easy 80-minute drive east from Melbourne, Victoria's spa country boasts the largest number of naturally occurring mineral springs in Australia, along with a large cluster of masseurs, beauty therapists and holistic practitioners. At last count there were more than 300 masseurs working in the area, evidence that rejuvenation is firmly on the local agenda.

Surrounded by mineral springs whose waters bubble out of the earth at every opportunity, Salus reclines on the sloping shores of Lake Daylesford, amidst magnificent gardens of tree fern, magnolia, Himalayan maples and pussy willow. A sparkling stream cascades beside the slate path leading to the spa's atrium-like glass entrance. Inside, all is light, airy and fresh. Featuring bamboo floors and blonde pine, cathedral ceilings, French doors and banquette seating covered in aqua suede, the design is refreshingly clean and the mood upbeat, a reflection of the great style and taste this family run establishment is famous for.

LEFT: All rooms at the Lake House have picture-postcard views over the surrounding lake, spacious gardens and bushland.

RIGHT: Private treetop spa cabins add a touch of adventure here.

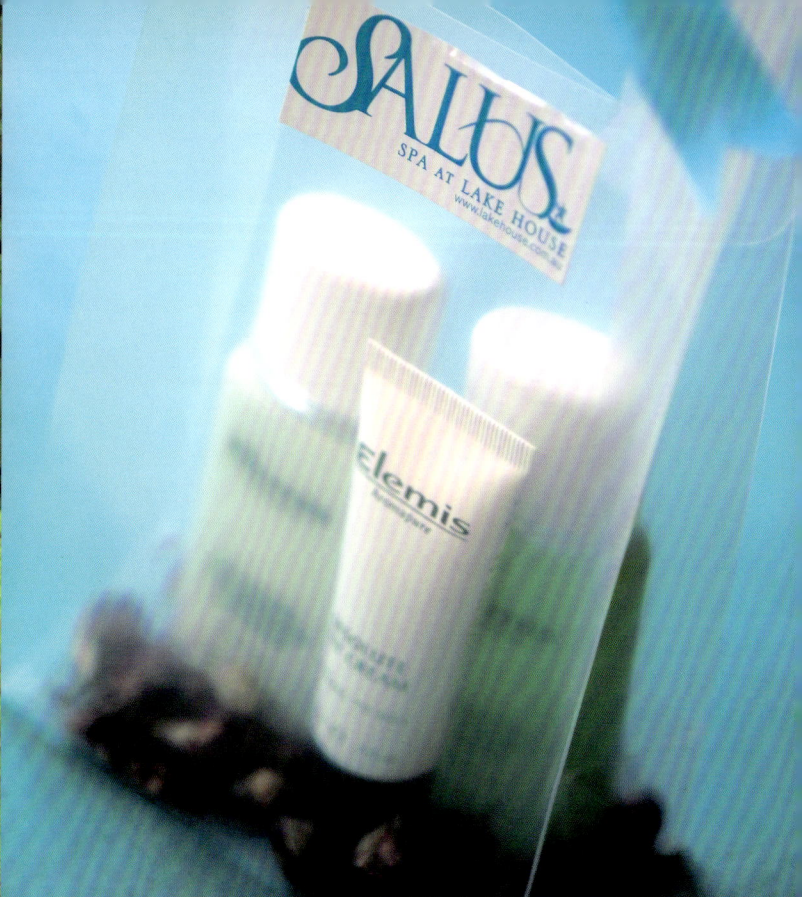

Salus has seven treatment rooms, including a large couple's suite with the ultimate hydrotherapy toy— the hydrostorm, (combining steam, waterfall, Swiss shower, aroma and colour therapy) and aquatherapy treatments are a natural feature of the spa. Each of the Elemis spa therapies offered begins with The Welcome Touch, a warm aromatic compress for the feet. This cleansing ritual aims to remove the urban environment, focus your senses and centre your thoughts. As the region is prone to water shortages, a steam and Vichy thermal cocoon was chosen over the traditional Vichy shower. The exotic lime and ginger salt polish I experienced in the cocoon left me beautifully cleansed, polished and softened—the perfect butterfly.

Complementing the mineral water, several detoxifying seaweed and ocean-inspired treatments are offered, including the Musclease Aroma Spa Ocean Wrap to help alleviate the pain of rheumatism, arthritis, muscle spasm and fatigue. Two cedar, treetop cabins over-looking the lake contain deep, Japanese-style tubs filled with hot mineral water and fragrant oils. From this special nest, guests can angle the louvered shutters surrounding them to obtain a bird's-eye view of the countryside.

Clear, effervescent and rich in minerals, the local water is nature's free dispensary of health and vitality. Every spring has a different taste, dependent on the mineral combination in the water. The Lake House have bottled their favourite, which

they offer to spa guests before and during treatments.

Guests here are warmly treated like part of the family and a generosity of spirit pervades all aspects of the property, which has an international reputation for excellence. Now I know why. I wonder if they'd adopt me?

Lyall Spa, South Yarra, Melbourne

Set beneath a leafy canopy in Melbourne's upmarket South Yarra, the Lyall Spa is conveniently close to the ritzy retailers of Toorak Road. The hotel has a devoted fashion clientele, mixed in with CEOs and travellers who like their hotels small, intimate and luxurious. Upon arrival, spa guests' cars are thoughtfully valet parked, before they enter the spa through the hotel's sophisticated foyer. An open fire blazes to the left, a champagne bar hums with the sound of South Yarra ladies lunching to the right.

Guests are directed to the rear of the hotel, through a set of glass doors into the narrow, two-storey spa, a veritable labyrinth of treatment rooms, a nail bar and banquette-style waiting area. A large glass of chilled water is offered and a lengthy questionnaire presented, to ensure that therapists know such things as the massage pressure you prefer, whether you are claustrophobic, recent medical history and even details of your skincare regime.

We are led further into the labyrinth. The tones of the spa are soft and sandy. Rooms are dimly lit with a quiet spa soundtrack in the background. It has a true sense of sanctuary.

The Lyall Spa's signature treatment is the Elemis Absolute Spa Ritual, two hours of decadence that starts with a spirit reviver and wellbeing massage, followed by a Japanese silk booster facial. My therapist uses an intriguing blend of massage styles influenced by Shiatsu, Hawaiian Lomi-Lomi, Thai and Balinese practices. Her deft strokes lead to the heart and the process has been known to have clients fast asleep in minutes—especially after the powerfully relaxing Thai foot cleansing ritual with hot lavender and chamomile infused towels is performed.

The proceeding Japanese silk booster facial, that includes a parade of beautifully sensory Elemis products— a cult English beauty brand (think La Mer meets Aveda)—is arguably the best facial treatment available in Australia. While your body is wrapped up, mummy-style, in warm towels, the face is given far more than the average clay mask and blackhead

ABOVE: The Lyall Spa's contemporary design lends a sense of space and tranquility to the premises.

extraction with products whose exotic ingredients include mimosa, honey, sea rocket, papaya and rose petals. The facial is performed to strict Elemis standards and includes the intriguing process of covering the face in a papery material made by silkworms that helps the skin absorb oxygen.

The treatment promises to have "immediate" results, something to be suspicious of, but my skin was thrilled by the ritual. The Lyall Spa's menu is very much about sensory thrills, with lime and ginger salt glows, strawberry herbal back cleanses, *chakra* balancing massages and muscle-easing ocean wraps. It also has a special "rituals" menu where guests can be treated like a Tahitian princess, with frangipani nourish wraps and detoxing regimes. There are Moroccan mud treatments followed by Swiss showers or dry body brushing to invigorate the skin. It is quite a spa menu.

Many of the Lyall Spa's local clientele have been known to book a room at the hotel after treatments, to make the most of feeling blissful in the Lyall atmosphere, rather than facing the world immediately after such decadence. I can't blame them.

THIS PAGE AND OPPOSITE: The Lyall Spa was one of the first to introduce the UK lifestyle range Elemis to Melbourne. The spa's fully-equipped gym, relaxation terrace, nail and beauty bar as well as other facilities and services are available seven days a week, with extended hours.

The Spa, Mansion Hotel, Werribee Park, Melbourne

There is something quite exciting about arriving at the Mansion Hotel and Spa. It has something to do with the possibility of seeing rhinoceroses, zebras, wildebeest and giraffes grazing peacefully in the distance as you drive onto the property. Next is the impressive scale, grandness and contemporary glamour of the hotel itself. There is a real sense of arriving somewhere special and a delectable promise in the air that one's expectations will be surpassed. A place of complementary contrasts—the Mansion is a fine example of blending the old with the new, both antique and modern, understated and bold, with yin-yang balance.

At the Mansion's doorstep are some of Victoria's greatest tourism treasures. Historic Chirnside Park Mansion and its 10 hectares of garden adjoins and encompasses this boutique hotel and spa, while the Victorian State Rose Gardens, Open Range Zoo, Shadowfax Winery, National Equestrian Centre and Polo Academy are all within walking distance. An exciting sculpture walk weaves through the grounds, which are filled with spectacular trees, many over 100 years old.

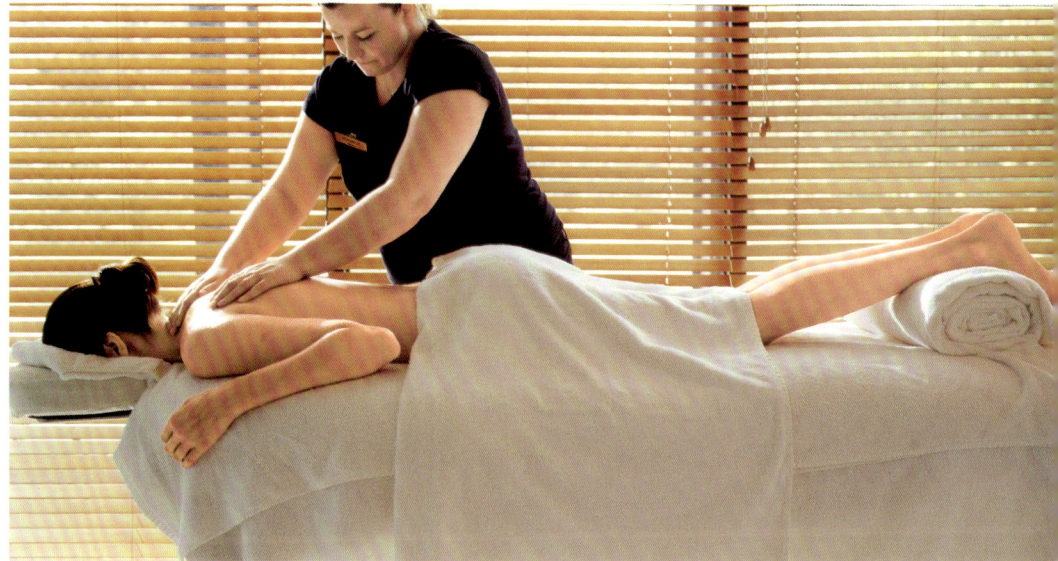

By the time I make my way to the spa I feel like a kid on Christmas morning who still has half his presents to open. I am not disappointed. Tastefully minimal, fresh and modern, the spa is also the gateway to a dramatically designed indoor pool and polished gym. The pleasing effects of simple details lingers—white orchids, groovy music

ABOVE: The Spa's various treatments are aimed at restoring the balance among the five elements that make up the human body and all things in nature—air, fire, water, earth and infinity.

and warm golden woodwork; bowls of apples, friendly staff, great magazines and spacious changing areas. The six white-tiled, multi-purpose treatment rooms are softened and given warmth by floor to ceiling hanging screens of gauze fabric, printed in colours that relate to nature's elements. Massages and beauty treatments for face, hands, feet and body also incorporate the use of the steam rooms, Vichy shower and spa baths.

A popular conference retreat and luxurious hotel of choice for many busy professionals, there is an emphasis here on providing a relaxing sanctuary and stress-busting therapies. The spa's goal is to design treatments that bring us back into balance, using nurturing touch and sensory experiences. At the root of this spa's holistic philosophy, drawn from multicultural, ancient and modern wellness rituals, are the five elements found throughout nature—air, fire, water, earth and infinity. When our elements are out of balance, the result is reflected in unhealthy skin and a lack of wellbeing in both the body and mind.

Before each treatment, guests complete an Aveda Elemental Nature questionnaire, which helps the therapists determine an individual's dominant elemental influence and the underlying causes of imbalance. Products, aromas and massage techniques are then customised to create personalised treatments and self-care rituals to bring immediate results, long-term benefits and enhanced wellbeing. It sounds like magic, but whatever you call it, this luxurious sanctum offers a cure-all to the malaise caused by stressful modern life.

LEFT, ABOVE AND PAGE 72: The delights of The Spa are myriad—chill out in comfort and with good conversation in the relaxation lounge, or for the more active, with a dip in The Spa's expansive indoor pool.

Park Club, Park Hyatt, Melbourne

Tucked away in a corner on the edge of Melbourne's central business district, the Park Club Spa is flanked by a cathedral, parks and stately buildings. Part of the Park Hyatt Hotel, characterized by Art Deco architecture and design, the spa is open to visitors and houseguests.

The spa reception features a curved wall of birch that curls away from the front desk like a conch shell. Spa guests are introduced to therapists in a café-style waiting lounge where treatments are discussed, herbal tea is served and a health questionnaire completed. The changing rooms are of marble and frosted glass, and include a stylish steam room, multi-head showers and a sauna. A grooming area with hair dryers and foldaway ironing facilities are provided for touch-ups before your return to the real world. Before, during and after treatments, clients may make use of the colonnaded, sandstone terrace surrounding the 25-metre edgeless indoor pool with

its mosaic wall mural, waterfall and domed ceiling. It's a glamorous spot to rest or enjoy a delicious spa lunch.

Artfully combining ancient methodology with modern techniques and facilities, the Park Club's holistic approach includes the use of organic and pure essential oil-based products. Cosmetic and therapeutic treatments, massages and tanning take place in six treatment rooms, which include a Vichy shower and hydrotherapy bath. Extra services include fitness and nutrition advice, lifestyle consultations and physiotherapy.

Enticing treatment packages, with names like The Hallucinatory and The Reverential are designed with renewal, vitality and wellbeing in mind. The Ultimate is an eight-hour affair that includes: a personal training session or herbal bath; salt glow treatment or body polish; herbal body mask with scalp treatment and eye wrap; full body massage; facial; pedispa; hand therapy; make-up application; eyebrow and lash tint with eyebrow shaping; a day pass to the training studio and therapeutic wet areas; nine hours parking; lunch and a gift.

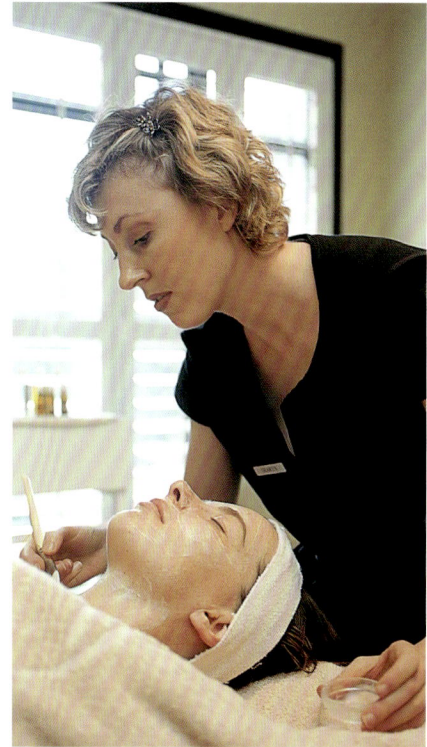

OPPOSITE: The Grecian mosaic mural is an unmissable feature of the Park Hyatt's indoor pool.

ABOVE: Enticing treatment packages are designed with renewal, vitality and wellbeing in mind.

Crown Spa, Crown Towers, Southbank, Melbourne

In terms of size, decadence and spare-no-expense luxury, the Crown Spa in Melbourne is without rival in Australia. Breathtaking in its opulence, spaciousness and attention to detail, the pampering here begins with the eyes, as the décor alone creates a sense of pleasant indulgence. So serene is the ambience that people lower their voices upon entering the domed, circular reception parlour, as if it were a place of worship. The air is rich with the promise that you will not leave this spa unchanged.

The tranquility is barely rippled as attendants in ivory-coloured silk *cheongsams* quietly lead the way to one of many beautifully appointed treatment rooms. The Crown Spa has an indoor 25-metre pool, spa restaurant, gymnasium, rooftop running track and tennis courts. Eastern and western treatments take place in five beauty rooms, two couple's suites, three pampering suites, two hydrotherapy rooms, Thai and alpha massage rooms and hair and beauty salon.

The Spa's impressive collection of contemporary Australian art provides a pleasant diversion not usually found in a spa. An elegant circular parlour with refreshment facilities and interesting books offers a luxurious place to relax, unless you are lucky enough to occupy a pampering suite, alone or with a companion, where there is ample choice of how and where to luxuriate.

Clients who book suites enjoy a private jacuzzi and steam room (fitted with a six-head effusion-type Swiss shower) for at least 30 minutes before a therapist returns to begin treatments. The luxury end of these softly lit suites includes twin massage beds, a sauna and large circular jacuzzi, steam room with Swiss shower, private lift access and a ceiling three stories high.

More than 40 therapeutic treatments are available, including a twin massage where two therapists provide a simultaneous massage; a clothed Oriental massage; various body wraps and polishes, hydro and thallasso therapies; hair and salon services and pure oxygen gas therapies.

Spa therapists are highly qualified and experienced. The nurturing soul who conducted my aromatherapy massage read my body like a fortuneteller reads a palm, offering some useful body maintenance advice at its conclusion.

A sophisticated enclave on the banks of the Yarra River in Melbourne, the Crown Spa is open to both hotel guests and the public.

ABOVE: The activity and relaxation oasis adjacent to this elegant spa includes a 25-metre pool.

OPPOSITE: The ceiling in this lavish "High Roller Suite" soars three floors above this lucky couple.

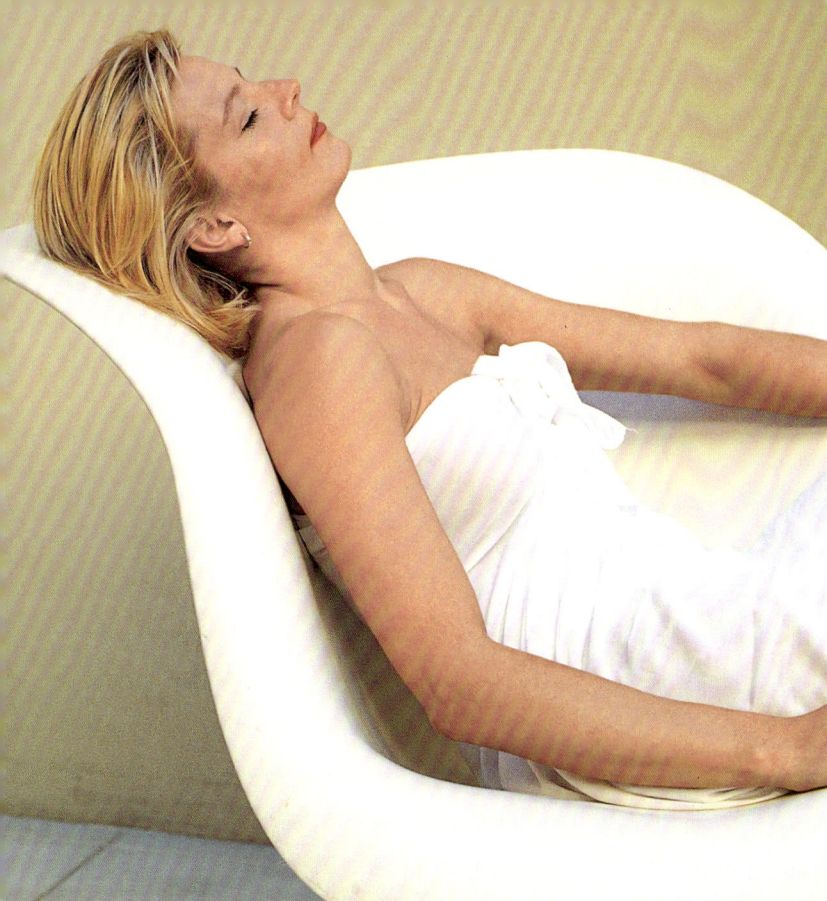

Aurora Spa Retreat, Prince Hotel, Melbourne

Perfectly situated to bathe in the first light of dawn, the eponymous Aurora is situated a stone's throw from St Kilda beach in Melbourne. Representing a blend of health, wellbeing and lifestyle, Aurora exudes a calmness and tranquility in all areas of its operation. It is the largest spa retreat in Australia, with 22 multi-functional treatment areas that are purpose-built for water therapies, wellness, body and skincare treatments.

Aurora's luxurious home is the ultra-chic Prince Hotel, whose hip designer style is balanced by Aurora's dedication to the heart of things, not the fashions of the day. Clients' needs are considered as a whole, taking into account exercise, nutrition, relaxation and self-awareness. Aurora's founder and director Lyndall Mitchell affirms: "It's all about balance—balancing our ambient, minimalist environment with genuine care and kindness, therapeutic body care, hydrotherapy, wellness and skincare therapies. We help our clients reach an optimum state of wellbeing so they are able to achieve their goals and enjoy the highest quality of life."

Discovering each client's goals is an essential part of the Aurora process; only realistic and achievable goals will have a sustainable long-term effect and result on lifestyle. Aurora ensures clients achieve their ultimate state of wellbeing and maintain this integral balance for the long term.

The path to wellness is paved with pampering, stimulation and enjoyment. Aurora's team includes naturopaths, acupuncturists, psychologists, Chinese medicine practitioners, yoga teachers and personal trainers.

Before a treatment, guests are shown to the time-out lounge where they can enjoy Aurora's herbal teas while listening to meditation music.

A couple's wet room, geisha tub and two steam rooms are used for Aurora's signature treatment, the Kitya Karnu steam treatment.

Aurora offers personally designed daily, weekend and week-long retreat packages.

FACING PAGE, CLOCKWISE FROM TOP LEFT: Soak your cares and troubles away in chic, peaceful comfort. One of Aurora's herbal tea blends. The Kitya Karnu steam treatment is a signature experience. Organic and indigenous ingredients are used in Aurora's products.
ABOVE: Splash out and spoil yourself with one of Aurora's nurturing and therapeutic treatments.

Natskin Spa at Immerse, Yarra Valley, Victoria

Immerse is all about the blending of life's greatest pleasures: food, wine, luxurious accommodation and fabulous pampering. Nestled among acres of fragrant, rose laden cottage gardens and grape-vines in Victoria's premium wine-growing region an hour's drive north of Melbourne, a visit to Natskin Spa is sure to delight all of your senses.

A new concept in wine lifestyle retreats, Immerse is a place where lovers of good wine and food can experience blissful spa treatments, or alternatively, where lovers of excellent spas can indulge in fine food and wine. Considering the spa, café and cellar door are in the same building this is quite easily arranged.

Natskin treatments are designed to beautifully pamper your body with goal-orientated results. Natskin's own goals are to provide everything you need to relax, rejuvenate and de-stress. The comprehensive consultation process prior to treatments also ensures that therapists can contribute towards any personal goals you may wish to achieve during

your visit, whether it be to relieve aching muscles, improve your skin tone or simply experience pleasure.

Hip simplicity and thoughtful professionalism are qualities that stand out at Natskin's Immerse spa. Everything looks good and feels right. A soothing water-wall feature in the spacious reception area fits well in a spa dedicated to renewal and cleansing. Wall-sized windows provide gorgeous garden views; the six custom-built treatment rooms are roomy and comfortable; and the long, deep blue bathrobes you will be offered to wear are plush and cosy. Only the best materials and furnishings have been used to create this tranquil, refreshing spa and every possible situation or guest requirement has been pre-empted.

Natskin's serene team of therapists are meticulously trained to provide treatments with a sophisticated approach to skin and body wellness. After completing a comprehensive consultation questionnaire beside an open fire in the plush relaxation lounge, guests are invited to read the latest magazines and sip fresh juice

ABOVE AND FACING PAGE: Natskin Spa offers a range of hydrotherapy treatments including the all-pampering, stress-busting aromatherapy steam infusion, and the ultimate in rejuvenation—a half-hour soak in Tasmanian red wine or cool milk.

or tea while their information is reviewed. Treatments can then be tailored to suit personal preferences and desired outcomes. Utilising her knowledge of aromatherapy, my therapist mixed an essential oil blend that best suited my physical state on the day itself. After a massage and an amazing mud-covered hydrostorm experience, another therapist noticed my skin was dry, and so applied some moisturizer for me. These rarely bestowed little extras speak volumes about this spa—I wish there were more of it. Therapists seem to have the confidence and encouragement to give that bit extra, to the benefit of all. As Natalie Ashton, the creator and co-owner of Natskin Spa says, "Therapists need

to have the freedom to meet every client's needs—you have to allow for some individuality, of both the therapists and clients. To see someone leave us happy after a wonderful spa experience, looking like a different person to the one who walked in, drives us to keep our standards high."

A natural beauty and massage therapist herself, Natalie opened her first spa in the Melbourne suburb of Ringwood 16 years ago. Still operating today, this spa was joined a few years ago by the Natskin Day Spa Retreat in South Melbourne. With Natskin at Immerse opening in 2002, the fulfilment of a long wished-for dream was realised. For the benefit of spa lovers everywhere, let's hope the dreaming continues.

ABOVE: Just a mere hour from Melbourne, Yarra Valley's countryside atmosphere is a sight for sore eyes suffering from an overdose of concrete.

RIGHT: Natskin therapists are highly trained both in the techniques of relaxation and body care. They are also renowned for their sensitivity to the needs of guests.

Breathtaker All Suite Alpine Spa Retreat, Mount Buller, Victoria

Australia's first alpine destination spa lives up to its name well. The views from its mountaintop position, are breathtaking and many guests here are taking a breather from hectic city lives. In summer or winter, the lure of the great outdoors in Victoria's high country is irresistible. Mt Buller is a popular skiing, hiking, mountain biking and abseiling destination, ensuring there is a regular supply of aching muscles and tired bodies to massage, soothe and nurture.

It may be cold outside and the snow may be piled high against the expansive windows, but it's always bikini weather inside. Breathtaker's large, open-plan relaxation and water-experience area feels something like a beach, only the sun lounges are set on sand-coloured tiles rather than the real thing. The sparkling, 20-metre lap pool is lined with blue mosaic tiles studded with gold and includes a secluded spa cave at one end, accessible only by water. Also in the communal area is

an enormous steam room with a central stone water bubbler, able to accommodate the apres-ski influx with ease. High in a wall beside the large circular spa pool, jets of water are aimed to tumble onto aching shoulders relaxing below. Opposite, a stone-enclosed wash-down shower features a 10-foot high, sunflower-size shower rose, the theory being

ABOVE: Nestled in its pristine alpine environment, it's no wonder this spa retreat is popular all year.

OPPOSITE: The spa is well equipped to ease the physical aches of strenuous skiing or hiking in enjoyable ways, such as a relaxing steam, soak or massage.

ABOVE: From relaxation massages, sports massages to treatments that stimulate lymphatic tissue, Breathtaker's spa menu offers a massage for every care and ache, delivered with expertise and gentleness. OPPOSITE: Water plays a huge role in this spa's aim to renew, revive and relax.

the higher and wider the shower head, the softer the rain of water which falls.

The Breathtaker is large, spacious and romantically lit, with two dedicated beauty rooms, a massage room, hair and make-up area, wet treatment room with Vichy shower, a hydrotherm cocoon, couples suite with twin geisha tubs and a combined geisha massage suite. The deep geisha spa tubs are lined with hundreds of air jets to aid relaxation, lymph gland drainage and blood circulation, while the underwater colour therapy lights promote a balanced mind and spirit. A rich colour scheme of black and gold echoes throughout the spa and contributes to an atmosphere of comfort, warmth and decadence.

In addition to pure essential oils, the spa uses products primarily based on marine extracts and salt water algae. Nourished by osmosis from mineral substances suspended in seawater, algae contains 10 times more trace elements than ground plants. These elements are transferred by osmosis to the skin's epidermis during treatments.

Carved out of the stoney mountainside itself, boulders and large rocks feature strongly in Breathtaker's design, which is based on the embodiment of the four elements: fire, water, earth and air. After these comes the fifth and highest element in ancient and medieval philosophy: the Quinta Essentia, which translates from Medieval Latin to "fifth essence." The element that explains the diversity and multiplicity of life and the finest or best of any substance, Quinta Essentia embodies the philosophies and goals of Breathtaker—to ensure you have the ultimate experience in comfort, quality and service during your visit to this excitingly located spa and hotel.

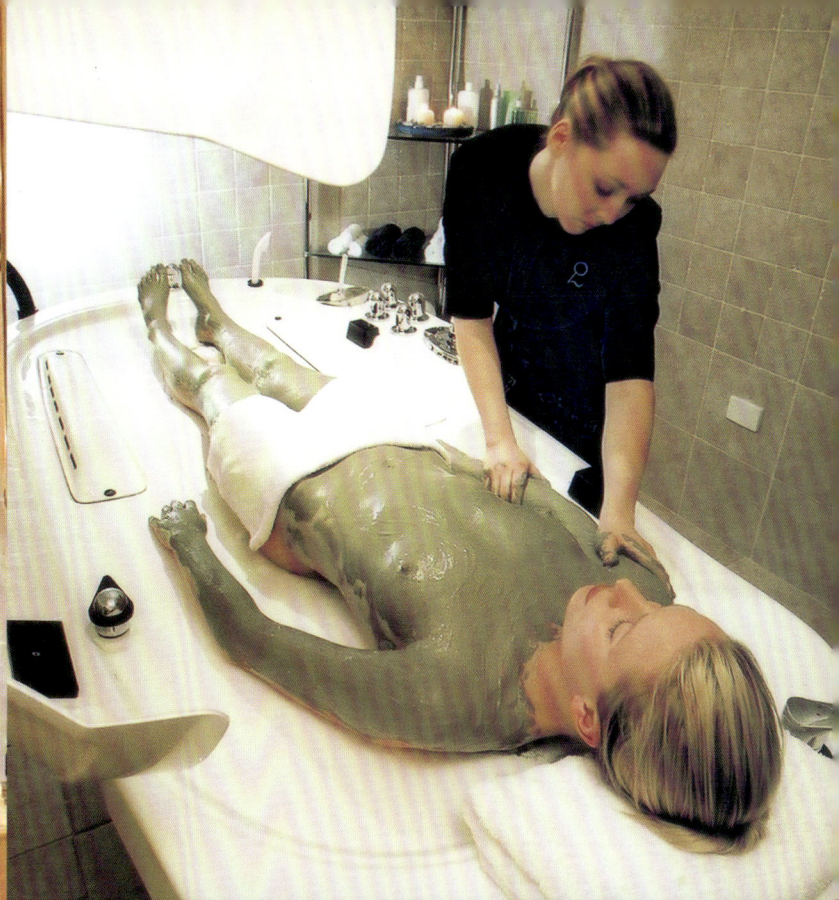

Waldheim Spa, Cradle Mountain Lodge, Tasmania

There is an almost tangible ancient magic at work in this extraordinary place. Visiting here is like stepping through the wardrobe in a C.S. Lewis novel or finding yourself at the door of Mother Nature's personal domain. The jaw-droppingly beautiful national park that encompasses Cradle Mountain is listed by the World Heritage Commission as one of the most precious places on the planet.

Located in the mountainous wild heartland of Northwest Tasmania, Cradle Mountain Lodge is named after the majestic mountain that can be seen from the lodge on a rare clear day. Misty, moss-covered primeval forests, vast button grass plains, soaring mountains and deep crystal lakes provide the spiritually uplifting setting for this contemporary wilderness retreat, comprised of individual wooden cabins and a central lodge and spa.

There's a good chance you will already be totally entranced by the rugged beauty of this living museum of wildlife, birds, plants and forests before you've seen the spa. Experiencing glorious natural wonders followed by glorious physical wonders seems to be the popular order of the day. Whether you visit after an exhilarating day hiking or some serious fireside relaxing, a luxurious treatment at Waldheim Spa will lead you to a place of dreamy peacefulness and deep relaxation.

Exclusively designed treatments with enticing names like Serenade of the Tasman Sea; Enchantment of the King Billy Forest and River Radiance use both local therapy products, many made with alpine ingredients, and Sodashi, a natural Australian skincare range chosen for its healing and nourishing properties. *Sodashi* is an ancient Sanskrit word meaning "wholeness, purity and radiance," qualities which form this spa's foundation. All treatments embrace this philosophy and passion and aim

LEFT, RIGHT AND FOLLOWING PAGES: Throughout their stay at Waldheim Spa, guests are constantly confronted by the breathtaking beauty of Cradle Mountain, a World Heritage Site.

to deliver therapeutic benefits as well as exquisite pleasure.

The spa's design is minimalist and sleek, and the sharp geometric lines contrast effectively with the soothing ambience. Large grey slate tiles, blond pine and diffuse recessed lighting complement the purity and pristine beauty of the wilderness outside. Upon entering guests are met by a large open fireplace set into a feature wall of river rock, a welcoming centrepiece to the lounge and reception area. Here, steaming cups of herbal tea are served in winter, while iced teas made from

locally-grown herbs are enjoyed during the summer.

There are six spacious therapy rooms, including a double Vichy shower room and steam infusion room. Many have a fourth wall made entirely of glass that provides panoramic views over the tea-coloured Pencil Pine River and eucalypt woodlands below. A popular relaxation area, known as The Sanctuary, includes a steam room, sauna, enormous open-air hot tub, cool plunge pool, and stylish white relaxation lounge.

As I left this spa, with a relaxed body and revitalised senses, the words of

ABOVE: Only 100 per cent natural products are used in all treatments at Waldheim Spa, and, combined with tried and tested techniques of ancient origin, promote "wholeness, purity and radiance" of body, mind and soul.

Cradle Mountain pioneer Gustav Weindorfer seemed to whisper through the trees, "This is Waldheim (forest home), where there is no time and nothing matters."

Empire Retreat, Yallingup, Western Australia

The Margaret River region of Western Australia is home to some of the best surf beaches and wine producers in the world, so as a glass of buttery chardonnay heads your way, think of it as the local tonic. Sophisticated and luxurious, informal and down-to-earth, Empire Retreat is designed to please the senses and to provide a space for some restorative pampering.

It is the wish of owners Jill and Perry Coleman that an interlude at Empire Retreat be as calming and indulgent as possible. Peaceful and private, the retreat is hidden within 110 hectares of farm pastures and bushland, studded with giant, native grass tree-bushes (*Xanthorrhoea preissii*). A plant of prehistoric appearance with a blackened trunk, glossy, mop-like head and protruding, seed-pod spears, these exotic natives create a protective moat around the central farmhouse and eight guest suites.

Blissfully spacious and stylishly appointed, your suite will be the venue for many sigh-inducing moments at the hands of local therapists. Massages, body scrubs, facials and other beauty treatments are available.

Each room has a deep spa bath, verandah and views of the surrounding bushland. Homewares and furniture sourced in India, Asia and Mexico complement the earthy tones of honey-coloured timbers and marble tiles. Sensuality was an important factor in choosing the beautiful bath oils and bedlinen and when planning the gardens, where wooden walkways meander through peaceful water gardens, filled with water-lilies and golden carp.

ABOVE: The outdoor spa hut shelters guests from the elements.
LEFT: One of the two hand-reared wallabies on the premises, a regular visitor to the Retreat.
OPPOSITE: Restorative pampering that is relaxed and informal.

Life here travels at a contemplative pace, assisted in no small way by a tranquil environment and beautiful climate. A thatch-roofed, garden daybed and jacuzzi cabana are great spots to stretch out and survey the landscape for resident wildlife— kangaroos, cockatoos and parrots, possums, lizards and two hand-reared orphan wallabies.

An hour's drive from the southern-most tip of Western Australia, this is a coastal region of natural beauty in every season: misty and wild in winter, languid and breezy in summer. The surrounding rural landscape includes many excellent walking tracks to towering Karri forests, limestone caves and a largely-deserted, cliff-buttressed coastline.

ABOVE: Slippers, robes and a basketful of essentials like bath oils are supplied for your use. ABOVE LEFT: Fresh marron, caught in the dam on the property.

RIGHT: A garden daybed provides an oasis for contemplation.

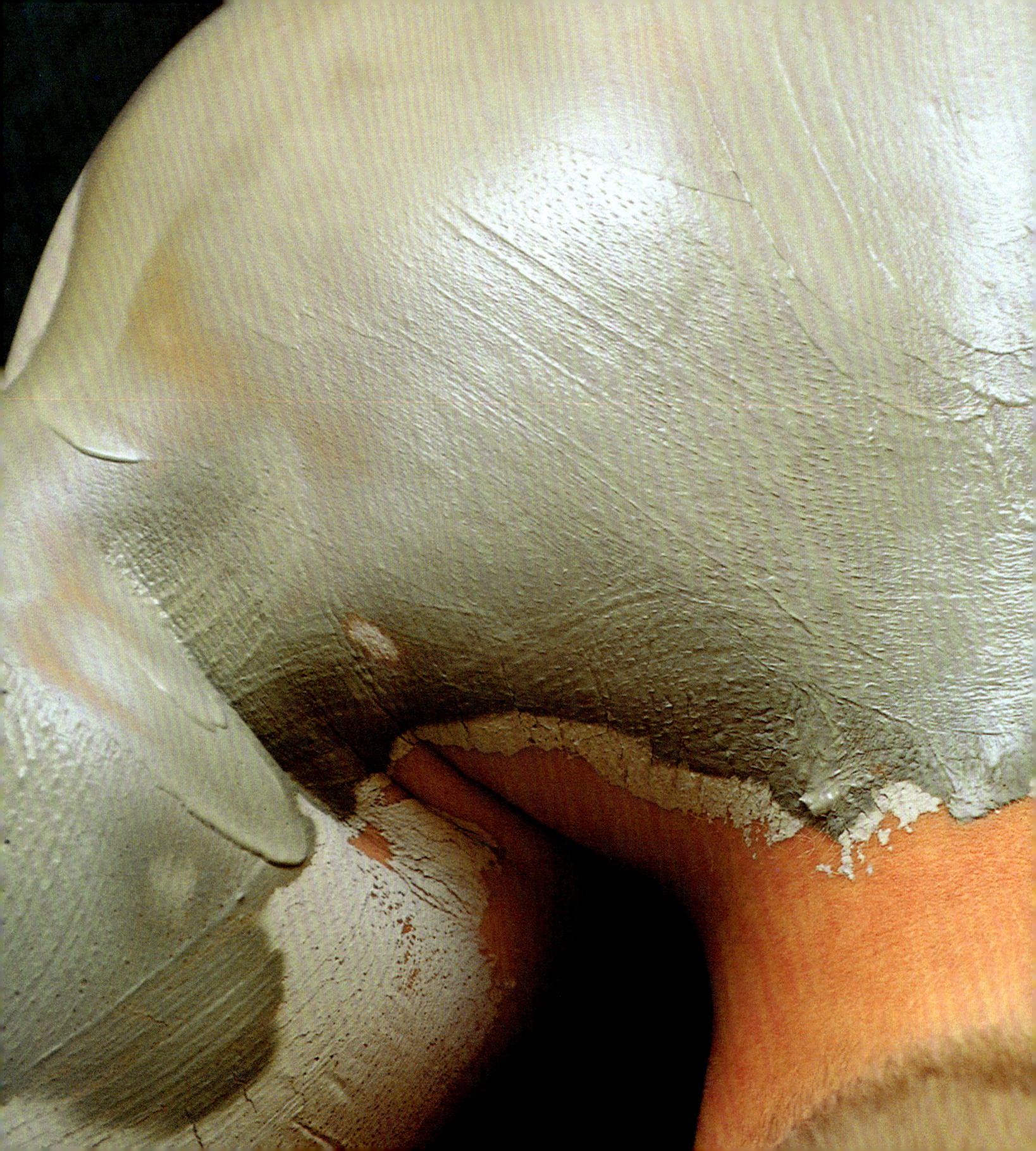

Australian Spa
Treatments

Skin Treats in the Heat

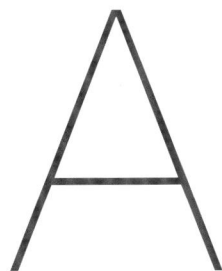

Australians love the sun. For many people around the world, "sunshine" and "Australia" are synonymous. Having fun in the sun is part of Australian life, but remember to slip on a T-shirt, slop on some sunscreen and slap on a hat. The sunburnt country produced many a bronzed Aussie before the risks and reality of permanent skin damage became known. The good news is that not all damage done to your skin is irreversible: if you give it some extra loving care it responds positively and quickly. If you get burnt, these relieving recipes from The Spa of Peace and Plenty will help to take the sting out of things.

Sunburn Soother

If you have overdone it in the sun, try this soothing treatment using that most adaptable plant—the coconut.

You will need one small growing coconut (identified by the coconut tree seedling growing from the shell—ask your greengrocer to source one!) and an hour or two out of the sun.

Crack the coconut and remove and discard the ball-shaped heart inside. Scrape the milky clear coconut jelly from the surface of the coconut flesh and rub onto the affected skin. The very high oil content of the coconut jelly soothes, moisturises and cools. Keep oil-coated, burnt skin out of the sun. Because the coconut jelly is quickly absorbed by the skin, there is no need to wash it off later.

Although very healing, this soothing recipe is not practical for many spa treatments. The Spa of Peace and Plenty provides the following in-house treatment for sunburn, which makes use of the abundant avocado trees and aloe vera plants cultivated on Dunk Island.

Sunburn Soother Wrap

A native of tropical Africa, the gel inside the aloe leaf has been used since ancient times to give instant relief from the pain of burns, wounds, dry skin and insect bites. An essential herb for home herbalists, this succulent thrives best in dry conditions and heavy shade. Over-watering and strong light discolour leaves.

Ingredients for sunburn soother bath
8 cups (2 litres) full cream milk
About 20 slices cucumber
A muslin bag filled with ½ cup (50 g) oatmeal and
   ½ cup (20 g) chamomile flowers

Combine all ingredients in a tepid bath and soak for a while. After getting out of the bath, place a plastic sheet on a table and lie down. Ask a friend to apply a light coating of 4 tablespoons avocado or vitamin E oil mixed with 7 drops each of geranium, lavender and chamomile essential oils.

Follow with a coating of the sunburn soother wrap.

Ingredients for sunburn soother wrap

1½ medium-sized avocado

2–3 tablespoons fresh aloe vera jelly

2–3 tablespoons yoghurt

Blend all soother ingredients together in a food processor until the mixture has the consistency of thick pouring cream.

Apply on the body and wrap your guest in plastic. Cover with light towels to allow the oils/avocado mix to be absorbed. While wrapped, apply the mixture to the face and place cucumber slices over the eyes. Massage scalp or feet during wrap time. After 20–30 minutes remove the face mask with a hand towel. Unwrap and remove any excess soother before showering. Finish by applying an aloe vera-based moisturiser to the whole body.

Taste of Tahiti Exfoliate

A great treat for your skin when the temperature is high, this colourful exfoliant is part of an exhilarating treatment at The Spa of Peace and Plenty. It is followed by a floral herbal bath, relaxing body massage and citrus body mist (a spray of purified water with orange blossom, witch hazel, macadamia nut oil, jojoba oil, and essential oils of orange and mandarin). We suggest you enjoy the exfoliate, and perhaps take a herbal bath after. Start with a skin brush and follow it with a full body mask of ripe papaya, fresh lime juice, mint and china clay. The enzymes in papaya and lime act as a powerful exfoliant and this

fragrant mix will leave your skin silky smooth and renewed.

Ingredients

½ ripe papaya, peeled and mashed

3 tablespoons clay-like kaolin (available from health-food shops)

3 drops of a cooling essential oil like menthol, peppermint or rosemary (or one of each)

1 teaspoon lime juice

Method

Combine all the ingredients. Brush your skin with a dry skin brush or loofah before applying the exfoliate to remove any dead skin and to prepare the skin to absorb the mixture. Apply the clay and papaya mix to the skin and cover the body with towels (this treatment is very cooling on the skin). Leave the mask on for 20 minutes. Wash off in the shower before stepping into a bath.

Ayurvedic Treatments

Ayurveda, the science of life, illness prevention and longevity, is believed to be the oldest and most holistic healing science in existence. This ancient art of healing has been practised throughout India for over 5,000 years and influences the philosophy of many Australian spas and their therapists.

Ayurveda emphasizes preventative and healing therapies along with various methods of purification and rejuvenation. In Ayurvedic medicine, all areas of human function can be divided into three *doshas*: *vayu* (air), *pitta* (fire) and *kapha* (water). Ayurvedic treatments aim to balance, nurture and harmonise the body and soul.

Ayurvedic Body Peel

Good enough to eat, and you'll know you've got this spicy mixture right if it smells like an Indian curry! All about the senses, this exotic exfoliate from The Spa of Peace and Plenty is inspired by the theory of *tridosha*, or the three *doshas*, the elements of material existence.

Ingredients for exfoliation paste
1 cup (100 g) chickpea flour (*besan*)
½ teaspoon cinnamon
½ teaspoon turmeric (has heating properties)
1 teaspoon cardamom
½ teaspoon ginger (has heating properties)
1 teaspoon fennel
1 teaspoon nutmeg
6 tablespoons crushed rice
10 drops sandalwood essential oil (has cooling properties)
1 tablespoon rose water (has cooling properties)
2 teaspoons sesame oil
Enough warm water to blend mixture into a thick paste

Mix all ingredients into a thick paste and massage over the body to exfoliate and balance the skin. Shower or rinse the mixture off. Dry well.

Ingredients for skin polisher
⅔ cup (150 ml) warmed honey
½ cup (125 ml) warmed full cream milk
1½ cups (150 g) grated cucumber

Apply warmed honey to the skin and massage into the body. Convert the sticky honey into a velvety texture by slowly adding 1 teaspoon warmed milk at a time. Massage into the body, then apply the cucumber. Coat both sides of the body and leave for 10 minutes. Rinse off and enjoy your naturally smooth skin.

Ayurvedic Shirodhara Treatment

The sensation of a continuous, rhythmic stream of warm oil directed onto the middle of the forehead can induce a blissful state of serenity and expanded consciousness. It is believed that oil stroking the "third eye" has a reflex-balancing effect on the deepest recesses of the brain.

Called Shirodhara, this is one of the most popular and effective Ayurvedic treatments. It has been used for thousands of years for ear, nose and throat disturbances, endocrinal imbalances, psychiatric disorders, sinusitis, epilepsy and headaches. Shirodhara also helps to strengthen *ojas*, the essence of fertility, virility, vitality and longevity.

Aurora Spa suggests this treatment at the end of a massage or facial. It takes 20–30 minutes.

Ingredients
4 cups (1 litre) warmed, cold-pressed sesame oil

Equipment
Table, large bowl and large funnel with a small hole or regulating tap

Method
Lie the person face up on a table and tilt the head slightly over the edge of the table. Place a bowl under the head to catch the oil.

Place warm oil into a funnel and position with the tap over the middle of the forehead. Ensure that the oil is not too hot. The oil should flow over the forehead, through the hair and into the bowl. When the funnel is empty, wipe the excess oil from the forehead and hair. The person should move slowly after treatment, and he or she should remain in a calm environment.

Note: If the flow of oil is too speedy, anxiety and nervousness will occur. If the oil is too hot, anger and heat will result. Oil falling from too far away can cause headaches, fever and agitation.

Macadamia Body Polish

Natural product guru Gayle Heron of Li'Tya (see page 187) uses macadamias in this natural body polish. Macadamia oil is the closest natural oil to our skin's oil, so it absorbs well.

Ingredients

12 macadamias, ground or crushed
2 sprigs dried lavender flowers
6 finely chopped eucalyptus leaves
½ tablespoon salt (for a gentler scrub, omit salt)

Method

Combine all the ingredients, then rub into the body, massaging well. Wipe body clean after, then rinse off in cool water.

Body Mud

Nutrient-rich muds have been used for centuries to soothe aches and pains, balance body systems and smooth the skin. This recipe from Gayle Heron uses green tea (a known antioxidant) and rosewater (great for dry, mature and sensitive skin). Used to soothe and revive tired skin, it is particularly good for acne, dermatitis and eczema.

Ingredients

1 cup (250 ml) green tea (cooled)
2 tablespoons kaolin
1 tablespoon rosewater
2 tablespoons macadamia oil
1 teaspoon Australian gum honey
2 drops each sandalwood, lavender and rose
   geranium essential oils

Method

Thoroughly combine all ingredients to form a paste. Smooth over the entire body and allow to set and draw for 10–20 minutes. Rinse off with cool water. Complete treatment with a scented massage oil or your favourite body lotion.

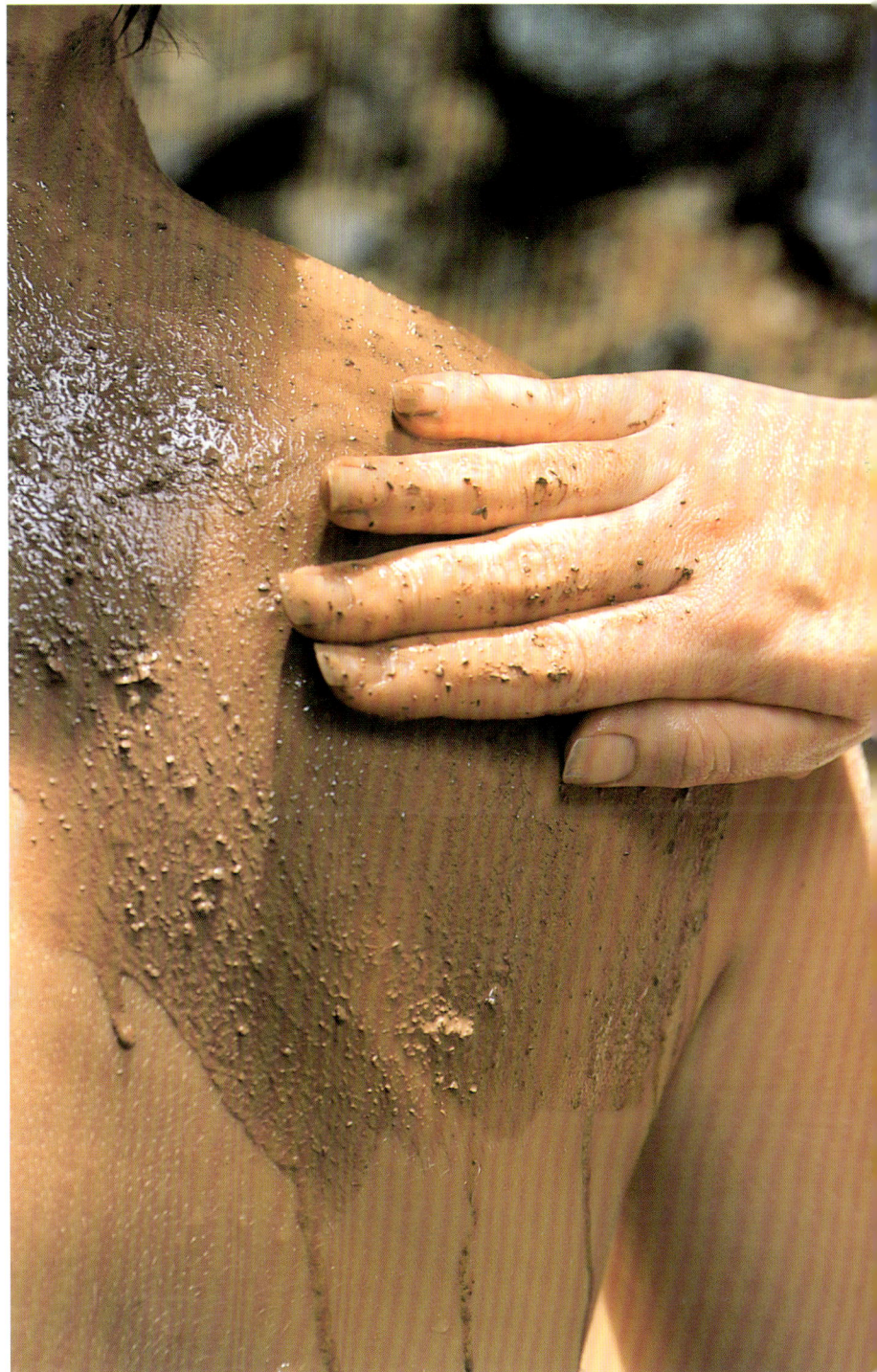

Body Scrubs

Skin is our body's largest organ of elimination. Good circulation to the skin helps the body remove toxins and enhances the secretion of moisturising natural oils. For centuries, various cultures have improved circulation to the body by creating friction on the skin. Known as exfoliation, it helps the blood and lymph systems to release waste and contributes to smooth, soft and supple skin. Island and seafaring cultures traditionally used sea salt, seaweed and the sun to improve circulation, while the Romans brushed their dry bodies with bristle brushes.

Body scrubs or exfoliates are an excellent way to stimulate skin circulation, cleanse the pores and remove the dead, scaly outer layer of skin. A body scrub should be mild and unabrasive enough for everyday use. As new cells are stimulated, your skin will take on a lustrous glow.

Sea Salt Exfoliate

When made to suit your skin type, this scrub by Janie Dallas-Kelly at Air Spa can be used instead of a cleanser. Here are quantities for two treatments. The mixture keeps refrigerated for 3–4 weeks.

Ingredients for normal skin exfoliate

½ cup (125 ml) sweet almond oil
1 cup (250 ml) aloe vera juice (available from the health-food store or supermarket)
1 cup (200 g) sea salt or coarse salt (Dead Sea salt from the health-food store is ideal)

½ cup (60 g) coarse rice flour
8–10 drops rose essential oil
½ teaspoon borax

Method

Warm the oil and add the aloe vera. Gently fold in the sea salt and mix until it forms a thick paste. Add the rice flour and stir well. Add the rose oil

and stir in the borax. Pack into an air-tight container and refrigerate.

To use, gently rub the mixture over the whole body from feet to waist and up to the heart, avoiding eye area. Leave on for 1–2 minutes then rinse off.

Variations

For dry skin, substitute rice flour for chickpea flour (*besan*).

For oily skin, substitute rice flour for barley flour.

For mature skin, add 1 tablespoon honey to aloe vera juice.

For blemished skin, add ½ cup (125 ml) thick yoghurt to aloe vera juice.

Australian Desert Salt Body Scrub

An invigorating treatment from Aurora Spa combining the best of Australian ingredients: salt from the Australian desert, lavender harvested in Tasmania, Australian bush flower essences, Queensland macadamia oil and the distinct aromas of the Australian bush—eucalyptus and tea tree oil. Salt has anti-inflammatory properties, remineralises the skin and reduces redness. It helps draw toxins out of the body through osmosis and encourages skin to secrete its natural oils. Lavender helps to restore balance, enhance relaxation, refresh, energise and promote healing.

This scrub is a stimulating exfoliate, and leaves the skin well nourished and smooth. It's ideal for rough, dry skin after summer suntanning or cold, dry winter weather and is a particularly good treatment for men. Do not apply to the face or on sunburnt skin, open cuts or wounds, after shaving or waxing, or to sensitive skin. Quantities make enough for one application.

Ingredients

½ cup (100 g) medium-ground Australian desert salt (or substitute with sea salt)

1 tablespoon crushed Tasmanian lavender (or any fresh lavender)

¼ cup (60 ml) warmed macadamia oil

1 drop each of lavender, tea tree and eucalyptus essential oils

7 drops each of Australian bush flower essences of waratah (helpful for coping with stress) and bottle brush (helps emotional bonding)

Method

Blend salt with the lavender. Pour the oil into the salt blend to form a slurry. Add the essential oils and bush flower essences and stir well.

To use, massage the salt mixture into the body, avoiding the face and sensitive areas. Pay particular attention to the heels, knees and elbows. Rinse off in the shower or bath, or leave on for 15 minutes in a steam room before rinsing.

Rockpool Salt Scrub and Soak

A favourite of Guy Vincent's, manager and formulator of In Essence essential oil.

The last three essential oils are Australian native species that display lovely qualities. The chemical composition of the blend provides calming, antibacterial, detoxifying and liver stimulant actions, to name a few. The aroma is magic!

16 drops lavender essential oil (*Lavandula angustifolia*)

8 drops ylang ylang essential oil (*Cananga odorata*)

20 drops lemon myrtle essential oil (*Backhousia citriodora*)

16 drops nerolina essential oil (*Melaleuca quinquenervia*)

8 drops blue gum eucalyptus essential oil (*Eucalyptus globulus*)

Method

Take a handful of sea salt and mix it with about the same quantity of Epsom salts. This is the base for an exfoliating salt rub or it can be dissolved directly into a warm bath.

Add the essential oil blend to about 30 ml (a shot) vodka and hand-mix through the salts. This will help with the even dispersion of the oils over the body or through the water.

To use, take some of the oil/salt mix and vigorously rub down the body to exfoliate and clean the skin. Then dissolve the remainder of the mix into a warm bath. For added effect throw some gum leaves, gumnuts and flowers into the bath water before sliding in. Add some soft candlelight and a glass of wine and it should feel like you are in your own private rockpool. Guy adds: "A friend told me to drop a few yabbies (Australian freshwater crayfish) in it for even more authenticity but that's just asking for trouble!"

Warning: These powerful oils can produce a burning sensation on sensitive skin. The citrus smells of the lemon myrtle are made up of aldehydes that are known to be reactive on the skin. In a bath the pores of the skin are open, increasing the chance of sensitisation. If you experience any problems, discontinue use and wash the area with fresh water. If the stinging continues, rub cold-pressed oil, for example sweet almond, on the area. Do not rub the mixture on broken or inflamed skin.

Fabulous Facials

Beautiful skin is the result of a well balanced diet, sufficient sleep, regular exercise and a skincare routine that works. Make the most of your natural assets. These recipes—using natural foodstuff from nature's store cupboard—will help improve skin circulation, cleanse and tighten skin on the face and neck.

Air Spa Face Pack or Body Wrap

This treatment, devised by Janie Dallas-Kelly, uses a variety of fresh fruit and vegetables. Their juices tone the skin and contain enzymes that help balance and cleanse the skin.

Ingredients
1–2 bananas, mashed
   (depending on the size of
   the area to be treated)
1 avocado, mashed
1–2 teaspoons oat flour
(from any health-food store)

For dry skin: Use 1 mashed apple, 1 mashed pear or 1 pulped nectarine, alone or added to the formula.

For blemished skin: Try ½ cup (125 ml) grape juice, 1 pulped tomato or the juice of ½ cup (65 g) cooked cabbage.

Method
Mix together well and in summer, refrigerate before application. Apply and leave on for up to 30 minutes. If using as a body wrap, slip into a pair of old pyjamas and relax before rinsing off.

Air Spa Basic Moisturiser

Another easy recipe from Janie Dallas-Kelly. It suits most skin types and will also protect skin.

Ingredients
3 tablespoons cold-pressed oil of your choice
2 teaspoons lanolin or cocoa butter
2 teaspoons rosewater
2 tablespoons aloe vera gel
5 drops essential oils of your choice

Warm the oil and lanolin or cocoa butter together. Add the rosewater and blend. Add the aloe vera gel and essential oil. Blend all ingredients together until it resembles a cream. Keep a usable amount in a jar and refrigerate the rest for up to 30 days.

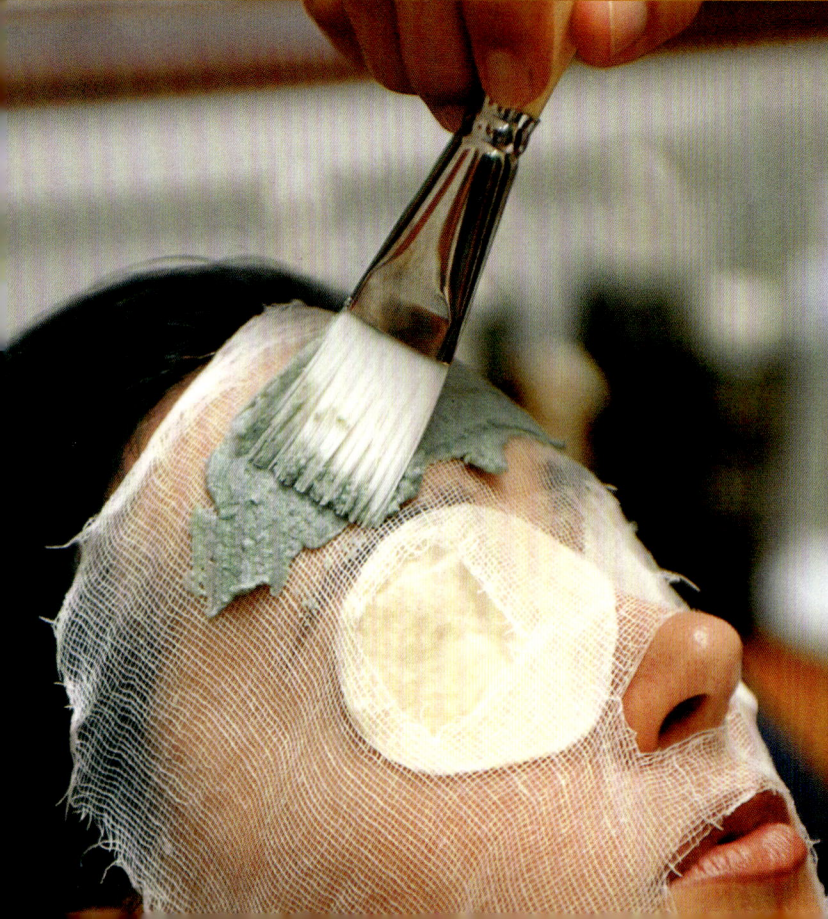

Anna's Mayonnaise Moisturiser

One for the chefs among us, this silky light moisturiser devised by Anna Kotz, medical herbalist and beauty therapist at Lilianfels, is made in a method similar to mayonnaise. This recipe makes about 2 cups (500 ml), but only lasts for one month in the refrigerator, so put some in jars and give to your friends. It may be used daily.

Ingredients

Oil component
2 tablespoons emulsifying wax (soy or lecithin based), available from the chemist or essential oil company
5 teaspoons macadamia oil
2 teaspoons beeswax
1 teaspoon tincture of benzoin (used as a fixative, adds colour and fragrance)

Water component
2 big cups (500 ml) chamomile tea
2½ teaspoons glycerine

Method

Mix the oil component ingredients together in a metal bowl. Place over a boiling saucepan of water or in a double boiler and heat to 70°C (160°F), until everything melts.

Brew the chamomile tea and allow to infuse for 15 minutes. Strain. Mix in the glycerine and heat the mixture to 70°C (160°F).

Pour the hot oil into a blender and mix, adding the chamomile mixture slowly. Turn the blender off and pulse for about 10 seconds every 2 minutes until the mixture cools. During this stage essential oils can be added. Use 12–15 drops (in total) of one or several oils of your choice. Anna's favourites are rose (great for sensitive skin), clary sage (a good hormonal balancer) and ylang ylang.

Foodie Facial Scrub

This exotic, aromatic exfoliating recipe from Anna Kotz at Lilianfels is also a cleanser. Orris root (the dried root of the white iris or *Iris florentina*) is sometimes seen as an old-fashioned ingredient, but it has a beautiful perfume and has been used by Italians for face and body powders for centuries. Geranium is an excellent skin tonic, astringent, circulation stimulant and soothes inflamed tissue.

Ingredients

1 tablespoon honey
2 tablespoons ground almonds
1 heaped teaspoon orris root (available from Eastern supply or incense shops)
1 heaped teaspoon sandalwood
3–4 tablespoons rosewater
5 drops geranium essential oil

Method

Mix the honey, almonds, orris root and sandalwood together in a bowl and add the rosewater little by little until you have a thick paste. Add the essential oil and mix.

To use, heap the paste into the hand and add a couple of drops of water to thin. Pat onto the face and massage gently into the skin. Remove with a warm, wet face cloth. The scrub will keep for a couple of weeks in the refrigerator.

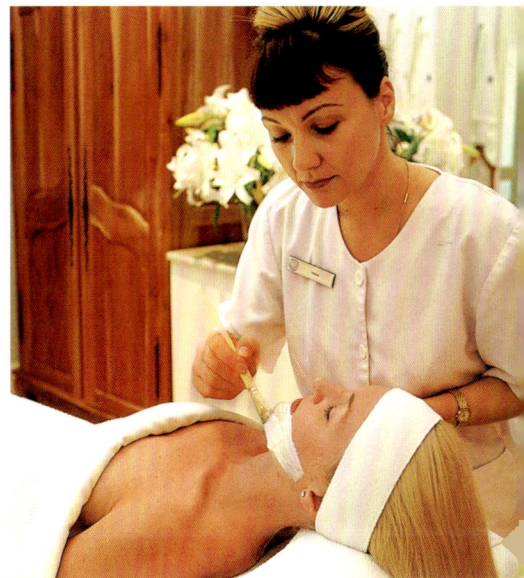

Australian Earth Aromatic Facial

All products come from the earth. Gayle Heron, the creator of a range of body care products based upon ancient knowledge held by the indigenous peoples of Australia, taps into the naturally powerful qualities of the Australian environment in many of her skincare recipes.

The native Australian ingredients that are used in this facial are available from boutique food suppliers. Lemon myrtle is a strong anti-inflammatory antiseptic, whereas wild lime is very high in vitamin C. A powerful antioxidant, vitamin C assists in the production of collagen and elastin, stimulating new cell growth.

Honey, used in the hydration part of this recipe, is a powerful antiseptic, nourishing to the skin and is known to kill bacteria and speed the healing process. Agar-agar is a gelatin-like substance made from nutrient-rich seaweed. Because we are talking *fresh* fresh, Heron recommends storing the ingredients in the refrigerator for up to five days—or simply giving yourself a one-off treat.

Cleanser

Ingredients

1 teaspoon finely chopped ginger
¼ cup (60 ml) green tea
¼ teaspoon lemon myrtle
½ teaspoon Australian gum honey (like stringy bark, blue gum, yellow box, red gum or iron bark)

2 wild limes, whole, or ⅛ of a normal lime, finely chopped
½ cup (125 ml) coconut milk
½ teaspoon macadamia oil
½ teaspoon agar-agar (from health-food stores)
3 drops lavender essential oil
2 drops lemon myrtle essential oil
2 teaspoons baked yam

Method

Combine all ingredients except the essential oils and the yam in a saucepan and cook for 5 minutes. Strain through muslin or a fine sieve. Keep the residue for the Exfoliant (see below). Cool until tepid. Add the essential oils (or oils of your choice), then add the baked yam and blend thoroughly.

Apply to the face and neck areas and leave for 10 minutes. Remove gently with a damp face cloth. Alternatively, just use vegetable oil.

If your skin is very congested or prone to oiliness, slice wild lime or pineapple and press gently onto it after removing the cleanser.

Steamer

Place 1 teaspoon dried lemon myrtle leaves or 10 fresh leaves and 4–5 fresh eucalyptus leaves (peppermint, lemon or other aromatic variety) in a bowl. Cover with boiling water and allow to cool slightly before steaming your face for 3–5 minutes.

Stimulating Exfoliant

Use grounds from the Cleanser (this page) and add ½ cup (50 g) finely grated carrot, 1 teaspoon dessicated coconut, 2 tablespoons natural yoghurt and 1 teaspoon kaolin (available from health-food stores). Combine and massage gently onto your face. Wipe off with a warm, damp face cloth.

Gentle Mask

Add 2 teaspoons dried lavender flowers and 1 teaspoon eucalyptus gum honey to 2 tablespoons full fat cream. Apply this nutritious, hydrating mix over face and neck and leave for 15–20 minutes. It can be applied to the body with a base of yoghurt or cream. Remove gently with a warm, wet face cloth.

Toner

Used to tighten pores and to balance the pH level of the skin, a toner leaves a smoother surface for hydrating. Use rosewater or the juice of ¼ of a normal lime or 1 crushed wild lime and add to 1 cup (250 ml) boiling water. Cool, place on a face cloth and apply to skin with gentle upward strokes.

Hydration

Ingredients

1 tablespoon macadamia oil
¼ teaspoon dried seaweed (any variety)
1 tablespoon rosewater
4 tablespoons coconut milk
½ teaspoon Australian gum honey
1 heaped tablespoon carrot peelings (rich in
    vitamin A)
1 teaspoon sesame oil
3 tablespoons water
3 tablespoons agar-agar
2 drops lavender essential oil
2 drops rosewood essential oil

Method

Combine all the ingredients except the essential oils in a saucepan and cook for 3–4 minutes. Strain through muslin or a fine sieve. Add the essential oils (or oils of your choice). Alternatively, complete the facial with a little light vegetable oil and blot with tissue. Very little hydrating is needed as the full cream is very nourishing.

Feet Treats

At the end of a long day many of us complain that our feet are "killing us." Yet, all too often, we expect them to endure the discomfort of high heels or ill-fitting shoes. With the miles they take you they deserve just as much, if not more, attention than other parts of your body. Treat your feet right and prepare any of these quick-and-easy foot pampering recipes from Janie Dallas-Kelly of Air Spa.

Mustard Foot Bath

Great on a cold night to warm you up, the mustard works to warm and relax tired feet, the spearmint refreshes them, the eucalyptus relieves aches and pains and the lemon myrtle is an antibacterial and fungus-fighting oil.

Ingredients
5 tablespoons mustard powder
2 tablespoons spearmint leaves
2½ cups (625 ml) pure spring water
5 drops lemon myrtle (*Backhousia citriodora*) essential oil
4 drops eucalyptus essential oil

Method
Make an infusion with the mustard, spearmint and water. Add the oils as you fill your foot bath with warm water (the water temperature to suit you).

Fizzy Feet

Create your own foot spa with this fun foot bath which will relax your feet and soften the skin for easier exfoliation.

Ingredients
2 drops essential oil of your choice, or try lemon and black pepper
½ cup (about 100 g) sodium bicarbonate
3 teaspoons citric acid (Berocca with vitamin C will do)

Method
Dissolve all the ingredients together in a bowl big enough to use as a foot bath and soak. Exfoliate afterwards, using your favourite foot file.

Foot Fetish

A wonderfully refreshing and cooling crème that soothes and gently softens this hard-working area of skin.

Ingredients
1½ tablespoons sweet almond oil
1½ tablespoons wheatgerm oil
2 tablespoons beeswax (unrefined)
30 drops spearmint essential oil
10 drops peppermint essential oil

Method

Gently heat the first three ingredients until they melt, then cool. When the mixture is lukewarm, add the essential oils. This makes about ½ cup (100 g) crème.

Massage onto feet and calves to soothe, refresh, cool and soften feet. Store any leftovers in a wide-neck glass jar and refrigerate.

Lemon Myrrh Foot Deodorant

Use this freshly scented spray first thing in the morning to put a spring in your step. The lemon deodorises, while witch hazel is an astringent that decreases the secretions from the sweat glands.

Ingredients
1½ tablespoons witch hazel
5 drops myrrh essential oil
5 drops lemon verbena or lemon myrtle
    essential oil

Method
Blend all ingredients together, store in an atomiser, shake well and spray regularly on clean feet.

Bush Foot Scrub

This is a stimulating treatment from natural product guru Gayle Heron. It uses native mint to help improve circulation and cool the feet; native thyme that is antiviral, antibiotic, diuretic, antiseptic and great for eliminating toxins; and rosemary, a physical and mental stimulant, muscle relaxant and antiseptic that alleviates problem skin. Lavender provides a divine scent and helps to restore balance, enhance relaxation, refresh, energise and promote healing.

Ingredients
2 sprigs dried lavender flowers
1 teaspoon ground native mint
1 teaspoon ground native thyme
1 small sprig rosemary, chopped
2 tablespoons vegetable or macadamia oil
1 teaspoon kaolin
1 tablespoon yoghurt
2 drops peppermint, sage and rosemary
    essential oils

Method
Combine all the ingredients and massage well into the feet. If possible, put your feet up for a while before removing with a warm damp flannel.

Native Flower Foot Soak

Another Gayle Heron recipe, this is an eye-catching, distinctly Australian, aromatic foot bath devised to relax your feet and soften the skin. The eucalyptus is probably Australia's best-known tree; what is perhaps less well known is that there are over 400 varieties of eucalyptus trees and shrubs and many have anti-inflammatory, antiseptic, antibiotic, diuretic, analgesic, deodorising, antiviral, stimulating and grounding properties. Try this foot booster for size.

Combine a blend of native flowers like grevillea, gum, banksia, native frangipani, tea tree (all high in nectar) with rose and lemon myrtle sprigs and aromatic gum leaves. Cover with hot water and cool until a comfortable temperature for feet to be immersed is attained. Sit back and soak for 15–20 minutes.

Finish the treatment with a vigorous towel rub to dry feet and massage with macadamia oil scented with a favourite essential oil.

Essential Oil Hair Care

As essential oils can enter the body through hair follicles, their use in hair treatments benefits our overall health. Apart from contributing to healthy, shiny hair, many people experience an increase in energy and clarity after an aromatherapy hair treatment as body heat continues to emit oils into the air. Essential oils naturally enhance hair colour, help rebalance the skin after hair has been chemically coloured, improve hair texture and appearance and smell great. Judith White, the Australian founder of the In Essence range of pure essential oils and author of seven aromatherapy books, offers the following tips and recipes in her book, *Aromatherapy Blends for Life*.

Hair Rinses

Use these rinses after your normal hair-care routine to impart shine and lustre to the hair and scent the head area, while providing a nourishing treatment to the scalp.

To make a rinse, add 1 drop of each essential oil to 4 cups (1 litre) water in a glass bottle that seals well. Shake vigorously and allow to stand for at least 24 hours for the oils to be taken up by the water. Shake again before pouring through the hair. Leave in and dry hair normally.

Lemon essential oil will rid the hair of residual alkaline after shampooing while sage has been known to disguise greying hair. Massaging the scalp with rosemary and juniper will stimulate and encourage new hair growth and improve circulation. Orange, mandarin and bergamot oils enhance red or ginger hair.

Dark hair blend: 2 drops rosemary; 1 drop sandalwood; 1 drop bergamot.

Fair hair blend: 3 drops lemon; 1 drop chamomile.

Anti-dandruff blend: 1 drop sage; 1 drop tea tree; 2 drops cedarwood.

Warm Oil Masks

If your hair is damaged, lacking lustre or feeling dry, a weekly warm oil treatment is a natural revitaliser. It replaces vital nutrients, makes your hair feel and look better, and feeds your scalp.

Blend these combinations into a base of ½ cup (125 ml) cold-pressed vegetable oil such as jojoba. Apply to dry hair, massaging well into the scalp and leave in for about 20 minutes. To maximise oil penetration wrap hair in a hot towel.

When removing the mask, shampoo must be added and worked through before wetting the hair. Wash thoroughly to remove oil, rinse and shampoo again.

Sensitive blend: 2 drops lavender; 1 drop bergamot; 1 drop sandalwood.

Oily hair blend: 2 drops bergamot; 1 drop sage; 1 drop cypress.

Damaged hair blend: 1 drop geranium; 1 drop lavender; 2 drops sandalwood.

Stimulating blend: 2 drops rosemary; 1 drop lemon; 1 drop cardamom.

Calming blend: 2 drops lavender; 1 drop neroli; 1 drop palmarosa.

Clarity blend: 2 drops lemon; 1 drop black pepper; 1 drop rosemary.

Scalp Massage Blends

The nutrients needed to build healthy hair reach the hair follicles through tiny blood vessels. When we are tense, head muscles contract, compressing these vessels and restricting the flow of blood. Regular scalp massage is one of the most effective ways to release muscle tension, condition the scalp and stimulate healthy hair growth.

Greasy hair: 20 drops bergamot; 10 drops cypress; 20 drops sage.

Damaged hair: 10 drops geranium; 20 drops lavender; 20 drops sandalwood.

Hair loss: 10 drops juniper; 20 drops cedarwood; 20 drops rosemary.

Dandruff: 20 drops eucalyptus; 10 drops cedarwood; 20 drops tea tree.

Aurora Ginseng Hair Treatment

This treatment improves circulation to the scalp and hair follicles, which relaxes muscle tension in the head and neck. It nourishes, lubricates and strengthens the hair roots.

Ingredients

Warmed hair crème conditioner (use one that is pure and unperfumed)

2 drops each of geranium and lavender essential oils

1 teaspoon ginseng in any form (tea, tonic or root from Chinese or health-food shops)

Method

Mix ingredients together and warm slightly in a microwave oven or in a bowl placed over a saucepan of boiling water for a few minutes.

Apply warm mixture to the scalp. Use a mask applicator or pastry-sized brush to apply, separating the hair into sections as you go. Massage the conditioner into the scalp with firm fingertip pressure over the entire head to stimulate pressure

points on the scalp. Brush the hair thoroughly with a large paddle brush, then cover the head with a hot towel, wrapping in a turban style. Leave on for at least 20 minutes, then rinse.

Air Spa Rosemary and Sage Shampoo Bar

This great shampoo for travelling comes from naturopath Janie Dallas-Kelly at Air Spa. It leaves the hair soft, shiny and extremely manageable. Makes 6 bars.

Ingredients
1 teaspoon dried sage
2½ cups (625 ml) pure spring water
½ bar Castille soap, grated
3 tablespoons vegetable glycerine
10 drops lemon essential oil
10 drops rosemary essential oil

Method
Make an infusion of sage and water. Add the soap and heat gently. Add the glycerine and remove from heat as soon as it has melted together. Add essential oils and pour into muffin tins to set.

Use very sparingly when washing hair, and rinse well. To store, wrap well and keep in the freezer for up to 6 months.

Air Spa Coconilla Shampoo

A fun cheat's recipe (it uses a manufactured product) that smells good enough to eat.

Ingredients
2 teaspoons glycerine
⅔ cup (150 ml) baby shampoo
20 drops vanilla essential oil
2 teaspoons coconut milk

Method

Blend oil with vinegar or juice.

Stand for a few minutes and massage into the hair. Leave for up to 10 minutes and rinse off.

Air Spa Cedarwood Treatment

Let the balance and peace of the forest envelop you with this special Cedarwood Treatment. Cedar is a potent cleanser that combats both excessively dry and oily scalps and rosemary can transform lacklustre hair into lustrous locks. Easy to prepare, this treatment makes ½ cup (125 ml) of lotion and keeps very well.

Ingredients
½ cup (125 ml) coconut oil
20 drops rosemary essential oil
10 drops cedarwood essential oil

Method
Melt coconut oil, add the essential oils, then mix thoroughly.

To use, warm a small amount in the palm of your hand and work into your hair. Wrap a warm towel around your hair and leave for 30 minutes. Remove, add shampoo to your hair and wash well. Rinse and style.

Method

Mix together and store in a cool place.

Use a small amount to wash your hair, and rinse well. Follow with Cider and Thyme Conditioner.

Air Spa Cider and Thyme Conditioner

A great hair and scalp tonic, this conditioner is good for dandruff too. Cider vinegar has a balancing effect on the pH balance of the scalp while sage is a masterful healer with many beneficial properties. As a variation you can add rosemary, bay or eucalyptus essential oils.

Ingredients
10 drops thyme essential oil
½ cup (125 ml) apple juice or apple cider vinegar

Massage—Secrets of Sensual Healing

s there a better way to bliss out, relax and repair our bodies than through the sensual touch of healing hands? Regular massages should be compulsory, or at least scheduled frequently into our lives. It would give to the world less stress-related illnesses and anger, and greater personal wellbeing. Regular treatments will also maintain the multiple health benefits massages bestow upon our bodies.

Therapeutic massages readily available in Australian spas and retreats include reflexology, aromatherapy, lymphatic, Polynesian Lomi-Lomi or Kahuna, deep tissue or sports, Reiki, Swedish, Shiatsu and head, hands and feet massages. Many therapists provide a combination massage best suited to individual needs. From a 15-minute de-stress scalp massage to a two-hour Lomi-Lomi affair, there are massages available to balance you, soothe you, speed you up or slow you down.

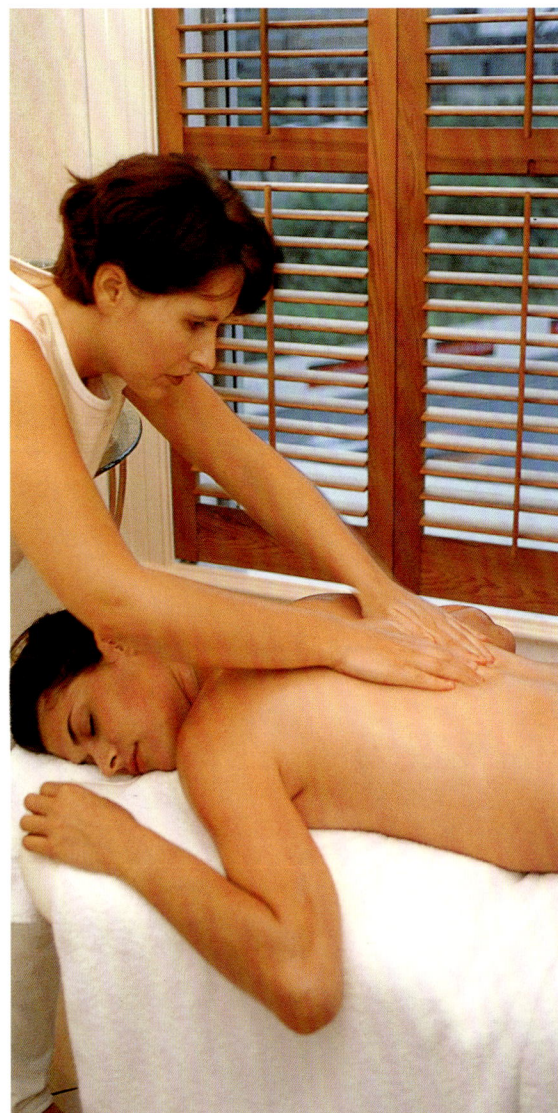

Shiatsu Massage

"Shiatsu" in Japanese means "finger pressure." The various techniques used in Shiatsu massage mostly involve firm pressure to various points and areas on the skin, known as meridian paths, *tsubo* or pressure points. While traditional massage soothes and relaxes tired muscles, Shiatsu works to balance and harmonise the energy, also known as *chi* or *ki*, which travels through our body's twelve meridians.

Originating in China sometime around 3,000 BC, Shiatsu was later developed by the Japanese and has been used as a simple home treatment in the Orient for centuries. A healing massage known for its ability to stimulate the body's capacity to heal itself, Shiatsu aims to remove energy blockages or tension within the body that could disrupt the free flow of *chi*.

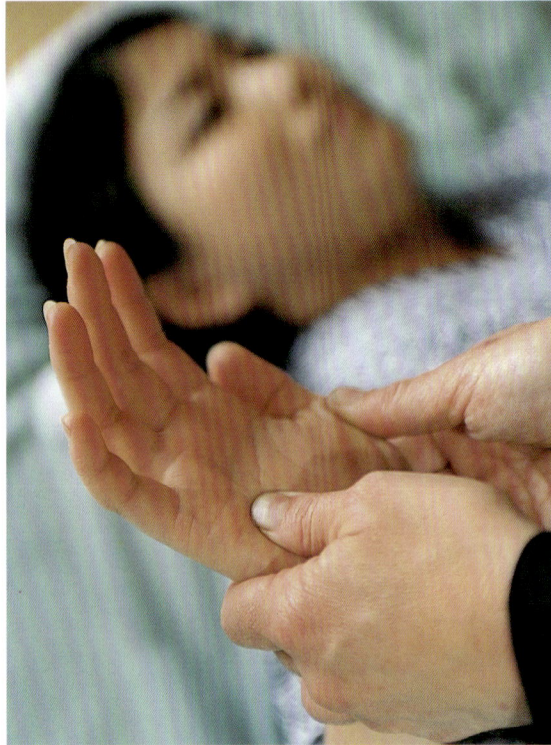

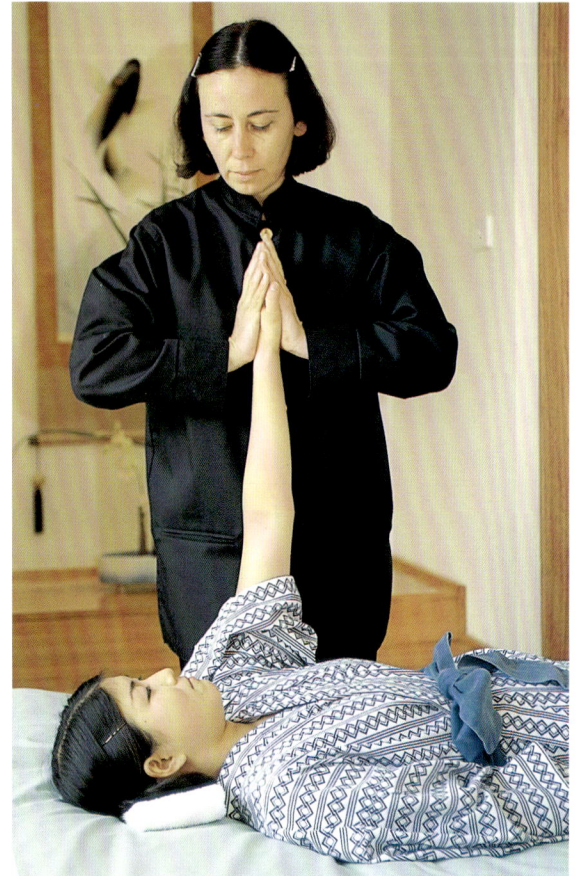

The practitioner uses fingers, hands, elbows, knees and feet to stimulate energy channels during Shiatsu. Techniques vary from subtle and supportive contact to dynamic pressure, including stretching, kneading, rubbing and pressing of the pressure points to relax the body and help energy to flow. Experienced practitioners can treat specific illnesses and stimulate individual organs, identifying where the body is unbalanced and blocked from the shape and formation of the body or by examining the face to determine where there is physical and emotional tension. Shiatsu is particularly helpful for stress-related illnesses, PMT, muscular pain, asthma, digestive disorders and poor circulation.

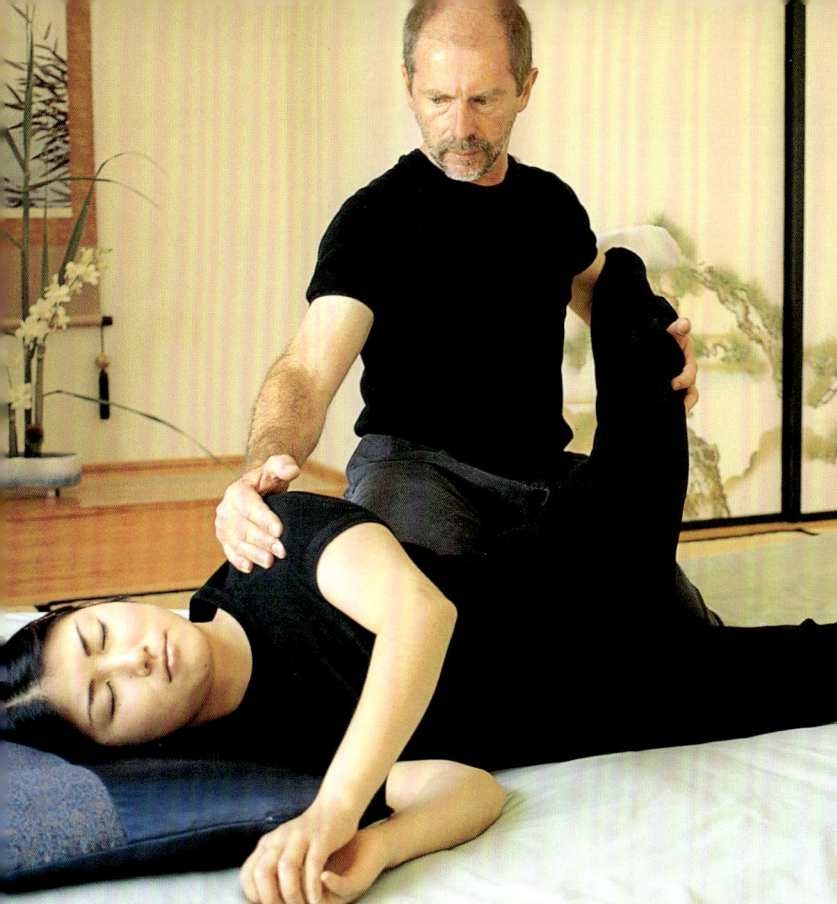

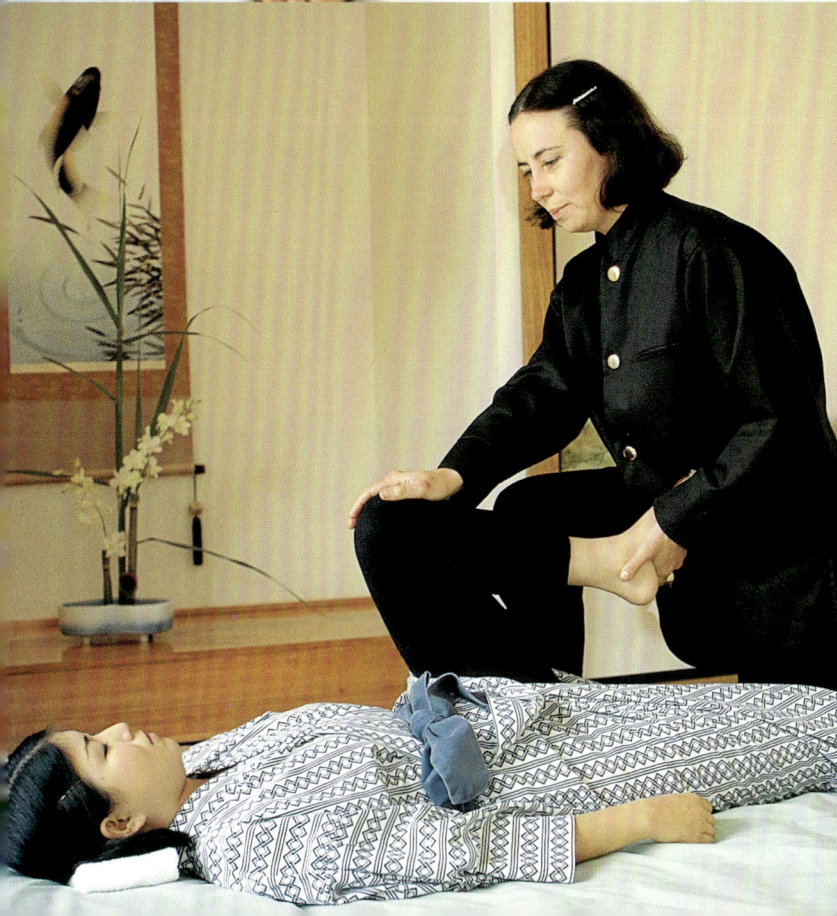

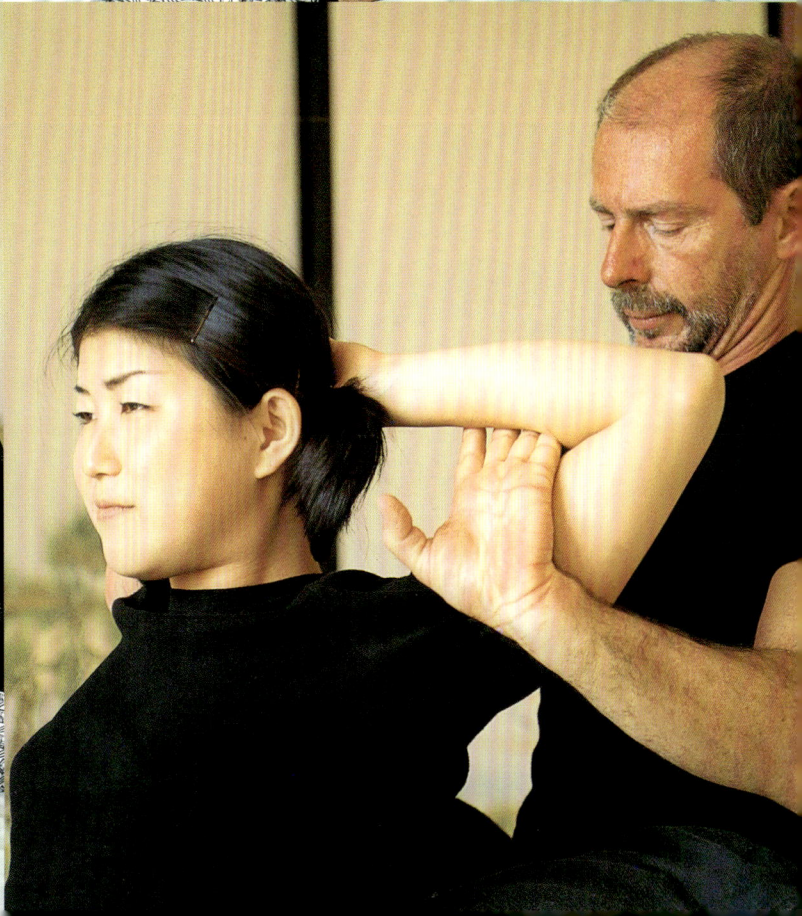

PEOPLE TODAY NEED NURTURING AND WANT A LITTLE BIT OF LOVING WITH THEIR KNOT CRUNCHING—THEY WANT TO FEEL THAT SOMETHING HAS CHANGED IN THEIR BODY AFTER A MASSAGE
— *JOHN ODEL*

Kiradjee Massage

"Kiradjee" means "healer" in the language of coastal Victorian Aboriginals. It is a word that applies to both the style of massage and to its creator, John Odel. Developed over the course of 15 years, Kiradjee incorporates techniques from deep tissue Swedish massage, pressure point work, peristaltic massage, joint mobilisation, aromatherapy and healing principles such as Reiki. Its aim is to give long-lasting benefits through the harmonious blending of these techniques.

Kiradjee is a uniquely Australian form of body massage. A holistic massage system with just the right combination of deep tissue work and gentle relaxation, Kiradjee is offered at the Regent Spa, Park Hyatt, the Joh Bailey Hair and Day Spa in Sydney, the Joh Bailey Day Spa in Melbourne and other venues by arrangement.

Deep and sensitive, as well as calming and healing, a Kiradjee massage lasts for a minimum of an hour and a half. When asked to describe the genesis of his massage style John explains: "After years of travelling and living overseas I began to realise that Australians as a race have an almost dream-like quality. Internationally we're seen as relaxed and happy, which may have to do with something our indigenous Australians believe—that the land influences the people and not the other way around. Every land has a vibration and after a while that vibration rubs off on its people. I think Kiradjee is very Australian. It's firm, it gets to the point, it's a very loving, generous and honest style of massage."

For the recipient, the difference from other massages is immediately clear. Lying face up on a low table, the treatment begins with a ritual meditation. Kiradjee therapists are taught to go into a meditative state before they begin the massage, drawing up the vibration of the land and focusing it through their hands. Breathing techniques and martial art floor exercises ensure therapists massage with their body and soul, not just their hands, and creative visualisation is used

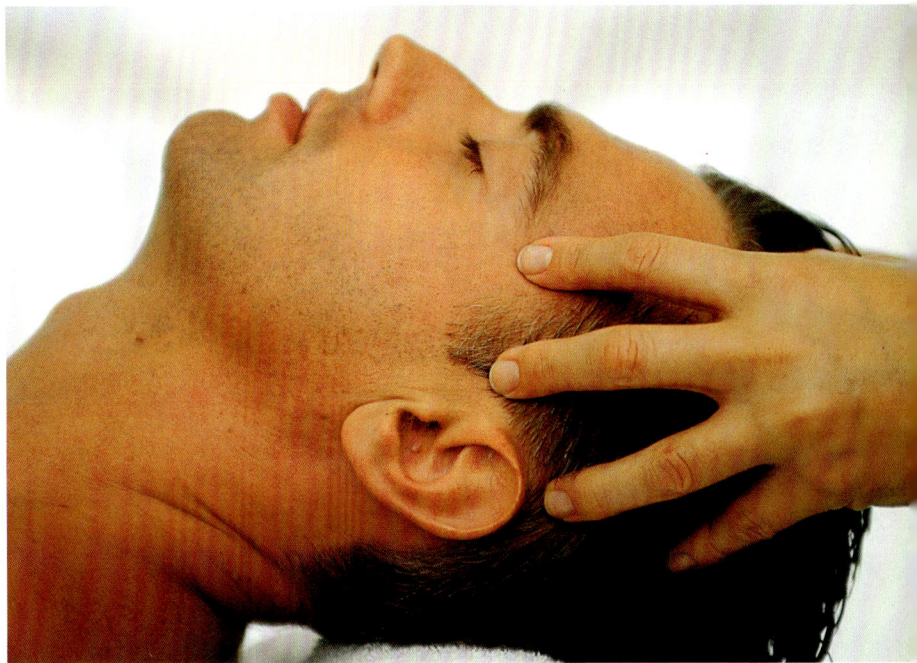

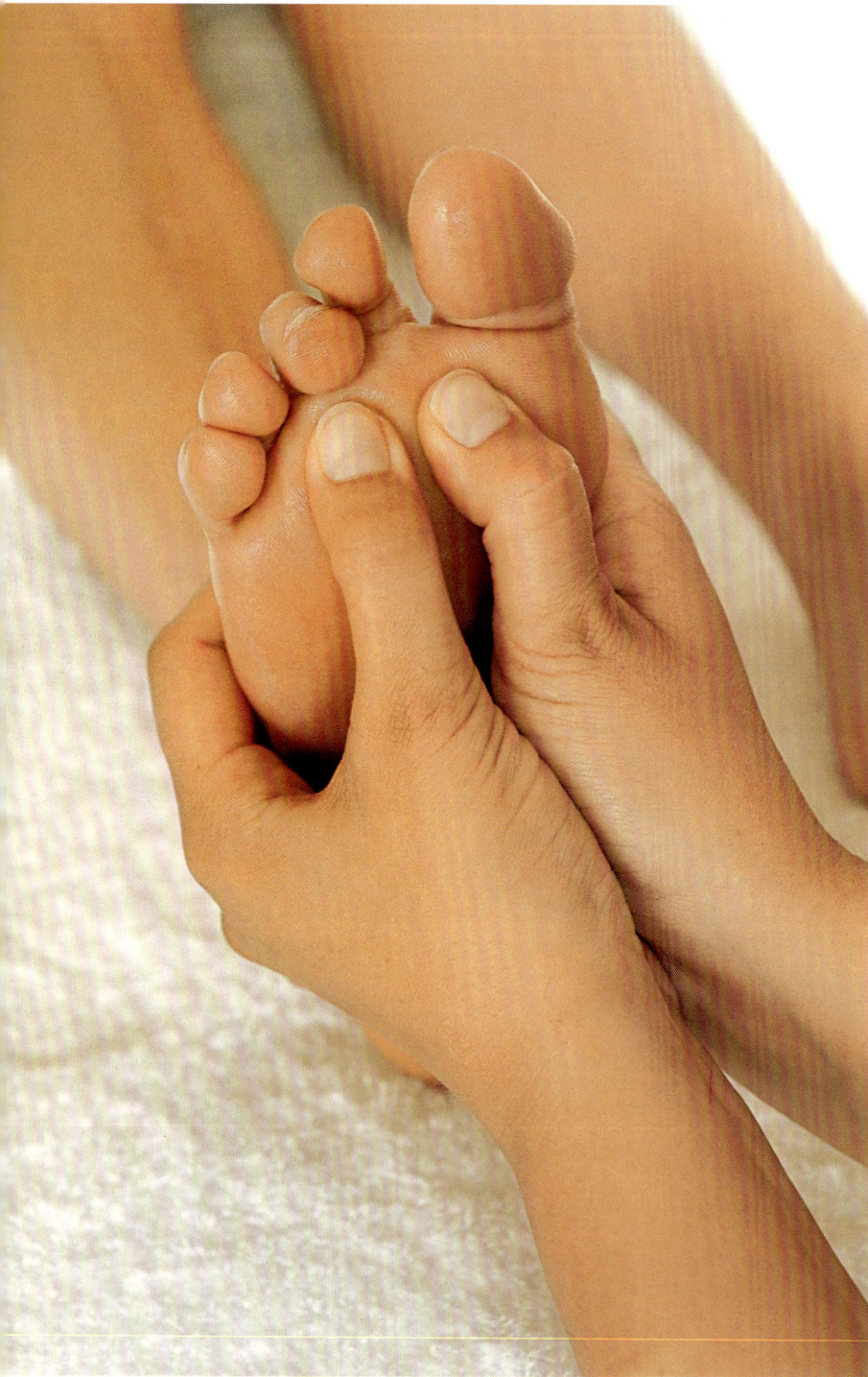

to help focus healing skills. The massage is then performed in a dream-like manner, with the table set very low.

A 20-minute neck and scalp massage using essential oils and warmth begins the relaxation process and familiarises the client to the therapist's touch. Using acupressure and pain-free deep tissue massage, muscles are relaxed and repositioned appropriately. Kiradjee involves a lot of work on the human energy field and on the spine. Deeper breathing is encouraged through a series of stretching movements and by the therapist pressing fingers between the shoulders. The massage follows a line foundation of decreasing patterns incorporating many circles and figures of eight, rather than a symmetrical pattern. Joint mobility work eases aching joints and reintroduces suppleness to the body's movements. The whole body is stretched and worked, with specific points manipulated to revitalise organs and release trapped energy. This freed energy increases recipients' awareness of their peripheral nervous system and contributes to a feeling of euphoria that may last for hours afterwards. The beneficial effects on the spine and body may last for days.

Odel has seen enormous changes in Australian society's attitude to massage since he began practising in the 1970s. He says: "Twenty years ago massage was frowned upon by insurance companies and by the medical fraternity. Only a handful of doctors would dare recommend a massage. Now they're more likely to say, 'You don't need four Valium—you're just stressed out. Go and get a massage and drink more water.'"

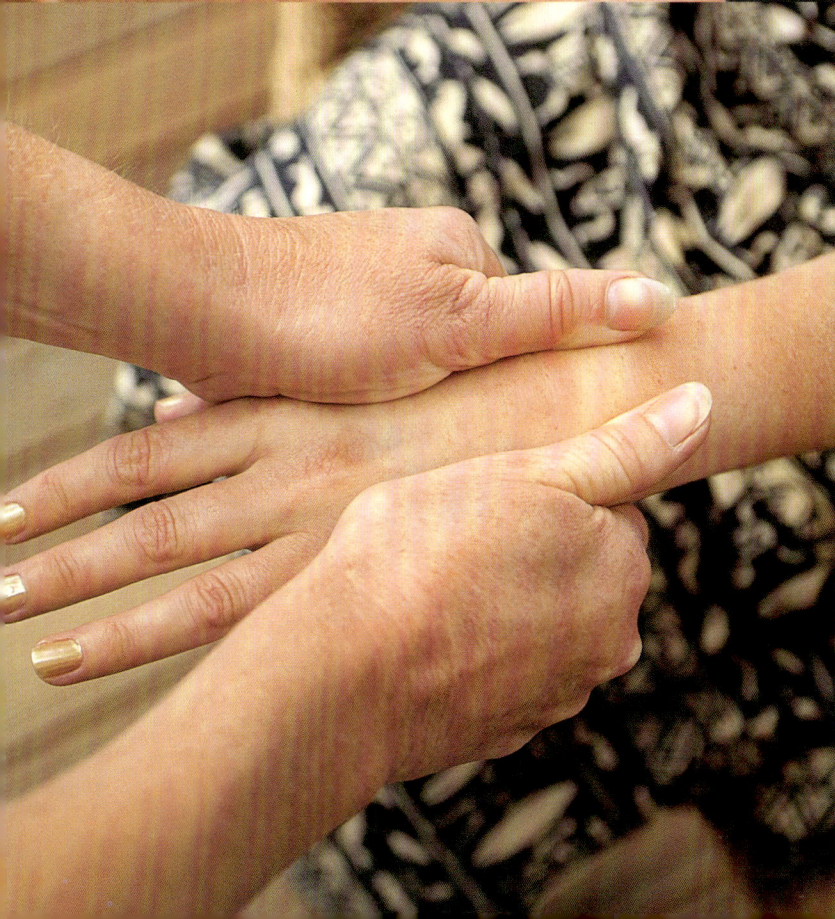

Secrets of Hydrotherapy

Water has long been recognised as possessing therapeutic, even miraculous, properties. From the seawater treatments used in ancient Greece to the healing mineral waters of spas in central Europe, ritual bathing for cleansing body and mind has always been a part of African, Indian and Christian culture. Even the word "hydro" (water) has long been applied to methods and places of healing.

Hydrotherapy refers to treatments using water in general. Varieties include balneo therapy or treatments using tap water; thalasso therapy, which uses seawater; or thermal therapy, using hot spring water. Many of the treatments available in today's spas have evolved from those developed by a nineteenth-century Bavarian priest, Sebastian Kniepp. He developed more than 100 treatment methods after recovering from tuberculosis by using water therapy.

As all life depends on its presence, it is appropriate that water should be such a valuable therapeutic medium. While we can live without food for weeks, our body tissues are composed of two-thirds water and dehydrate quickly. From a hydrotherapy point of view, water also provides the transport for waste products to be expelled from the body. Every day our sweat glands pump out about 3½ cups (900 ml) of water. About one-twentieth of this weight is nitrogenous waste matter. One of the benefits of hydrotherapy is that it increases the efficiency of the sweat glands. Both stimulating and relaxing, hydrotherapy beauty treatments can protect against illness, relieve stress, stimulate sluggish circulation and improve body metabolism.

Water temperature is an important element in hydrotherapy. The greater the difference in alternating water temperatures used during a treatment, the better the effects will be. Heat applied to the skin draws blood to the surface temporarily, while cold water has the initial effect of driving it away. The lasting effect is of warmth, since, by the laws of action and reaction, blood must circulate back to the vessels and tissues it came from.

Most spas these days have wonderfully sophisticated equipment and technology to provide the simultaneous benefits of different water pressures and temperatures. At home, however, we can recreate basic hydrotherapy baths and showers using cold water, hot water and alternate hot and cold water. Consult your doctor before taking any strenuous treatments, and remember a couple of Kniepp's golden rules.

Cold water should never be applied to a chilled body. Have a warm shower or exercise gently first.

Remove excess water with your hands after treatments. Towel-dry only areas of the body that

won't be covered by clothing. Wrap up warmly in natural fibres, allowing the skin to breathe.

Go for a short brisk walk after cold treatments to generate body warmth. After warm baths, tuck yourself in bed for at least half an hour and rest.

Cold Water

A short application of cold water has a toning and invigorating effect on the body part treated. Due to the contraction of the small blood vessels, a tingling sensation is accompanied by the skin going slightly paler. Shortly after, the skin glows pink. This is caused by the dilation of small arteries in the skin.

Fill a bath to a depth of about 25 cm (10 inches) with water no colder than 16°C (60°F). Lower your hips into the bath and splash water over your chest. Stand and run on the spot (carefully) for a few seconds. The whole process should take between 30 seconds and 2 minutes.

Cold baths should be avoided by people suffering from heart conditions, general weakness, nervous tension or anaemic conditions. The use of a non-slip bath mat is recommended.

Hot Water

Hot baths are generally enervating and increase the efficiency of the sweat glands. They should be at least 38°C (100°F). When heat is applied to the skin, nearby arteries dilate and the blood slows, while at the same time more blood is pushed into the charged arteries, causing redness and congestion. If the heat is not removed the blood becomes locked and perspiration occurs.

The skin's opened pores effectively absorb the active constituents of any herbal and medicinal preparations. Seaweed, peat, sea salt, essential oils, Epsom salts, soda and sulphur can be added to hot baths to treat problems ranging from arthritis and poor circulation to muscle fatigue.

Alternate Hot and Cold Water

Alternate hot and cold baths act like an artificial pump to stimulate blood flow and venous and lymphatic drainage. They can bring about a rapid reduction of inflammation when applied to congested areas of the body. They are also useful when there is a need to increase local circulation. The general rule is 2–3 minutes in hot water followed by 30 seconds in cold water. Repeat three times and finish with the cold water.

Neutral or Warm Baths

From uplifting your spirit to providing deep relaxation, a purely soothing soak can work wonders. With a water temperature of about 36.7°–37.2°C (90°–95°F), bath treatments, or balneo therapy, can and should last longer than hot baths. Adding relaxing herbs and essential oils enhances the effect of a regular bath. Make yours more blissful with these simple suggestions from Janie Dallas-Kelly at Air Spa.

Herbal Bath for Sound Sleep

Ideal for the stressed out, this relaxer works on mind and body simultaneously with the minimum of effort.

You will need chamomile, meadowsweet and valerian tea bags from a health-food store and half a lime, sliced.

Make a pot of tea in 2 cups (500 ml) water using all of the above. When sufficiently brewed (about

5 minutes) pour into a container. Using fresh tea bags, refill teapot with boiling water.

Fill the bath at your favourite temperature and add your "tea." Pour yourself a mug from the teapot and slip into the bath. Add 5 drops of lavender essential oil for extra stress relief if desired.

Oily Skin Treatment Bath

Ingredients
5 drops basil essential oil
3 drops rosemary essential oil
3 drops May Chang or lemon essential oil

Method
Add to warm running water, then soak blissfully.

Normal Skin Treatment Bath

Ingredients
5 drops neroli essential oil
3 drops rose essential oil
1 cup (250 ml) soymilk
1 tablespoon honey

Method
Add to warm running water, then soak.

Dry Skin Treatment Bath

Ingredients
6 drops rosewood essential oil
6 drops bergamot essential oil
2 tablespoons sesame oil
1 tablespoon honey

Method
Add to bath water, and feel your skin replenishing.

Coolum Spa Herbal Bath Ball

A fragrant bath ball of herbs that makes enough for two baths. The oats soften the water, draw impurities from the skin and leave it soft and smooth. Geranium emits a perfume that is calming, balancing and uplifting. Mint relaxes the muscles and citronella eases muscular tension and is beneficial during times of stress. The herbs can be fresh or dried. A few drops of essential oil can also be added to the bath water.

5 tablespoons oats
5 tablespoons lemon balm leaves
5 tablespoons scented geranium leaves
5 tablespoons mint leaves
5 tablespoons citronella leaves
5 tablespoons lemon verbena leaves

Place the herbs on a square of porous cloth, like muslin. Pull the corners together and tie with an elastic band or ribbon. Place the herbal bath ball into a hot bath to infuse for about 10 minutes before you hop in.

Thalassotherapy

From the Greek word "thalassa," meaning "sea," thalassotherapy incorporates a variety of therapeutic treatments using seawater, such as baths, body wraps, underwater massage and pressurised water jets. Seawater is full of essential minerals and an abundance of trace elements and organic substances that medical research tells us can restore and preserve good health. Salt (sodium chloride) is the dominant mineral in seawater; others include magnesium, calcium, sulphur, potassium, bromide, silicum, iron, copper, aluminium and zinc. The sea is also rich in biological elements and is a plentiful reservoir of seaweed, plankton and marine bacteria. A potent healer in its own right, seaweed is believed to reinforce the immune system, contain antibiotic elements, stimulate the thyroid gland and encourage the body to burn fat.

The first thalassotherapy centre was founded at Roscoff in Brittany, France by Dr Rene Bagot. He discovered that the trace elements and minerals in seawater were similar to those in blood plasma and could be absorbed through osmosis into our bodies, especially when the water was heated to body temperature.

Thalassotherapy is so effective that a bank of information and research into the effects of seawater and seaweed on a variety of illnesses—called the Federation of Sea and Health—has been set up in France by orthodox medical doctors.

Seawater and seaweed treatments are used extensively in Australian spas to cleanse the body of toxins, stimulate circulation and revitalise, firm, tone and refresh the body and skin.

Aromatherapy Pick-me-ups

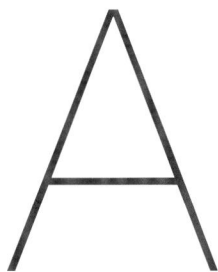

Although its roots can be traced back to early Egyptian, Indian, Chinese, Greek and Roman cultures, a therapy that utilises essential oils is relatively new as a healing discipline in its own right. The term "aromatherapy" was coined in 1928 by a French chemist, Rene Maurice Gattefosse, who started serious research into the healing powers of essential oils after burning his hands in a laboratory explosion. Immediately after the explosion he plunged his hands in some pure lavender essential oil and found they healed extraordinarily quickly, leaving no scar.

Following the work of other pioneers in Europe, two important figures emerged in the field, making considerable contributions to the study and development of aromatherapy: Margeurite Maury and Dr Jean Valnet. Valnet was a medical doctor who experimented with essential oils and recorded the results, bringing credibility and authority to the practice and publishing numerous books and articles on the subject, among them the classic reference book, *Aromatherapie*. Madame Maury, an Austrian biochemist, developed methods of applying the oils to the skin with massage and is the author of *The Secret of Life and Youth*, another aromatherapy classic. Valnet was orthodox in his approach and prescribed oils to be taken orally, while Maury attempted to treat the whole person—mind, body and psyche. Micheline Arcie, who studied under Maury and Valnet, combined their techniques to create a modern aromatherapy technique that is now used by therapists around the world.

Aromatherapy is the art and science of treating human illness and creating and enhancing mood with essential oils. It can be used to heal through inhalation, massage and through oral administration (under the supervision of an experienced therapist or doctor) in herbal infusions or in cooking. A holistic therapy, aromatherapy treats feelings and spirit with the same care as the physical body. It can be used to invigorate and stimulate, or to soothe and calm, to improve concentration, to inspire, to arouse, to cleanse and to cool.

Aromatherapy combines two basic primitive senses, touch and smell, using them to boost the body's defence mechanisms.

Aromatherapy helps to restore the balance between body, mind and the outside world—a harmony that is continually disrupted by pollution, stress and the rigours of modern existence. Aromatherapy can also cure a multitude of ailments, from flu and colds to aches and pains. It can help with sleep problems and repair damaged skin. As essential oils are valuable antiseptics (their aggression towards germs is matched by their total harmlessness to healthy body tissues), they can also help to fight infection.

NATURE KNOWS EXACTLY HOW TO HEAL US, SO WHEN YOU CONSCIOUSLY HARNESS HER VAST STOREHOUSE OF INTELLIGENCE YOU BRING BALANCE TO YOUR ENTIRE BEING
— *NIKKI GOLDSTEIN*

The lifeblood of aromatherapy is pure essential oil. Essential oils are the volatile substances that give plants and flowers their characteristic smell, preserve their moisture balance and protect them from insects. They are secreted by special glands and stored in tiny sacs found in the leaves, petals, berries, fruit, stems, bark, resin and seeds of plants. Culled from the very essence of the plant, they are scented and powerfully potent. Essential oils have the ability to alter mental and emotional states because they affect the hormones and the chemistry of the brain, as well as work on the more subtle energies of the body such as memory, feeling and awareness.

The process of extracting oils is an art in itself and requires infinite patience. Over 300 jasmine blossoms are required for 1 tablespoon of oil, while the petals of 30 roses yield a single drop of rose oil. Each flower must be hand-picked before the sun becomes too hot on the first day the flower opens.

The tiny molecules in essential oils are dynamic, active and highly sensitive. When inhaled or massaged into the skin they quickly penetrate into the bloodstream and body tissue. Although they do not remain in the body for more than a few hours, they may trigger a healing process that can continue for days or weeks.

Australian spas use the power of aromatherapy in many treatments. Most use essential oils in burners or vaporisers to create and complement mood and ambience; many use products infused with essential oils; others ask clients to smell several oils and choose one that will be used throughout a treatment. Invariably people select the oil they need, rather than a personal favourite.

Nikki Goldstein, Australian author of *Essential Energy: A Guide to Aromatherapy and Essential Oils,* believes the reason why aromatherapy has become so popular nowadays is because "People need feel-good therapies in their lives—treatments that make them feel positive, uplifted, revived and happy." She continues: "Aromatherapy is also a profoundly sensual practice. It awakens the senses and stimulates all systems of the body. Being touched and enveloped in heavenly scent can make you feel nurtured, soothed, bathed in pleasure and cared for. And the miracle of aromatherapy is it works instantly, anywhere, and at any time."

How to Use Essential Oils

Purity Australia, an Australian company that produces a range of pure essential oils called "The Oil Garden," provide the following advice for ways to introduce essential oils into the body:

Massage: For both the body and face, mix 6 drops of essential oil to every 2 teaspoons (10 ml) of carrier oil.

Bath: Add 6 drops to a warm bath and soak for 15 minutes.

Inhalation: Add 6 drops essential oil to 4 cups (1 litre) steaming water. Cover the head with a towel and steam for 5 minutes while inhaling vapours.

Vaporisation: Add 6 drops of essential oil to a vaporiser.

Direct application: Never use undiluted essential oils on the skin or ingest them internally without a doctor's advice.

Compress: Add 6 drops essential oil to 4 cups (1 litre) water. Place a soft cloth over the surface where the essential oils tend to float. Lightly squeeze out the excess moisture and place on the skin. Use cold water for sprains, bruises and headaches; warm water for skin treatments and hot water for boils, arthritis, abscesses as well as rheumatism.

Aromatherapy Facial

A facial is often a fast track to relaxation and is also great for your skin. Essential oils possess anti-ageing properties and have a beneficial affinity with the skin's molecular processes, making them perfect for a "home spa" treatment.

This step-by-step aromatherapy facial has been adapted from Australian aromatherapist David Wehner and is reproduced with the kind permission of Nikki Goldstein.

1. Clean the face and remove all make-up. A multipurpose liquid soap or olive oil and glycerine, is ideal. Milk on a moist cotton ball will also clean the skin and remove make-up.
2. Make a compress by dropping 2–3 drops pure lemon or lavender essential oil in very hot water and immersing a small towel into the water. Wring excess water and, while still steaming, gently wrap face in the towel, patting it down over the face. This simple hydration process performed regularly (ideally every morning) will help balance the skin, reduce the formation of blackheads and refine pores. Men find this treatment softens their whiskers and makes shaving easier. It also aids people with breathing problems or colds and flu.
3. Remove the towel when it is cooling and pat the face dry with a clean cloth.
4. Spritz the face with a gentle astringent such as witch hazel or a floral water made from distilled water with lavender, rose and neroli essential oil added.
5. Apply a gentle scrub to the face, neck and decolletage. Mix 1 tablespoon ground almonds

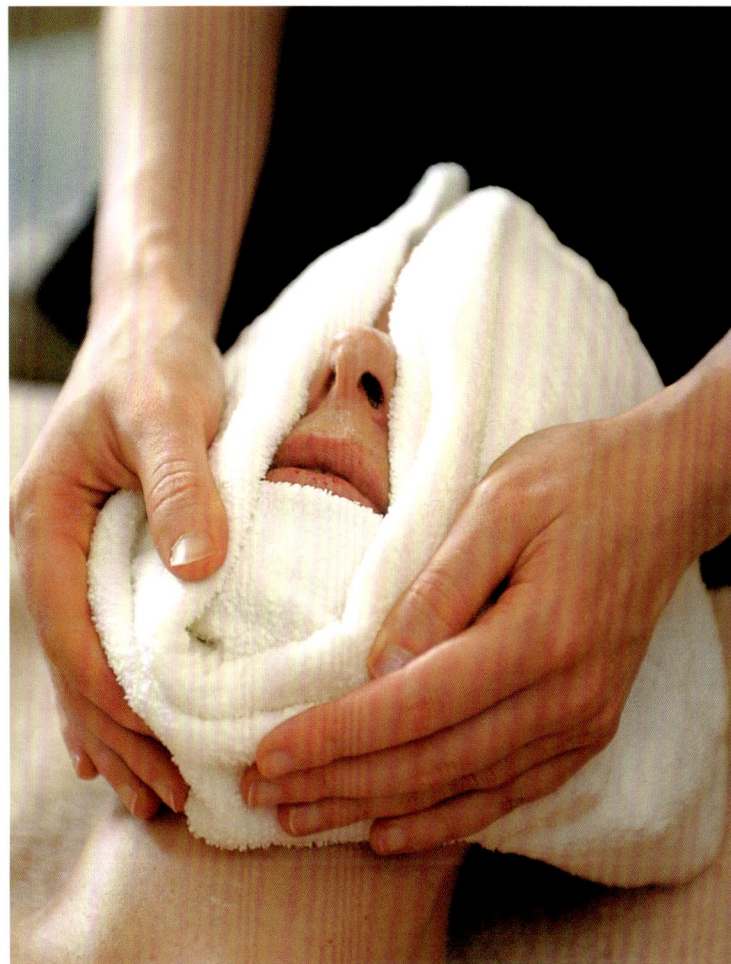

with 1 teaspoon natural honey (a powerful antiseptic and a good healing agent). Apply in gentle circular movements. Allow to dry for 10–20 minutes, then rinse off with warm lavender water.

6. Apply a mask made from powdered green clay. Clay powder is available from many health-food stores and can be mixed with witch hazel, water and essential oils. A drop of peppermint essential oil will help to clear blemishes and revitalise dull complexions, while a drop of lavender will soothe and calm sensitive or irritated skin. Alternatively, mixing a drop of mild oil such as chamomile, rose or geranium to the mask will boost any skin type.

7. Finish by moisturising the skin. Dampen skin with warm water before applying the moisturiser. Blend carrot oil with equal amounts of evening primrose oil and vitamin E oil. If you like, add a couple of drops of rose, lavender or neroli essential oil to this formula.

Carrier Oils

Any substance that can "carry" essential oils into the body is known as a carrier oil. Air is a carrier and so is water. All aromatherapy skin creams, shampoos and body products are simply carriers that enable the essential oils contained in them to be absorbed by the skin. The most frequently used carriers are cold-pressed vegetable oils, which act as natural and nutritious vehicles and dilute essential oils.

Author Nikki Goldstein has the following practical advice and information about creating your own mood therapy essential oil blends:

The best carrier oils are fresh vegetable oils that have not been chemically treated. These oils are more perishable than supermarket oils and should be checked for rancidity. Once opened, they are best kept in the refrigerator.

Essential oils will last between three and six years, except for citrus oils, which deteriorate between 12 and 18 months. Sensitive to sunlight, essential oils and blends will stay fresher in either dark blue or brown bottles. Plastic can be degraded by essential oils, so store your blends in dark glass bottles away from sunlight.

The ratio of essential oil to carrier oil should be 8–12 drops of essential oil for every 3 teaspoons (15 ml) for baths or massage. For facial blends, most aromatherapists will use 6–8 drops to every 3 teaspoons (15 ml). If in doubt, err on the side of caution and drop only small quantities of oil into your blends, or perform a patch test on the forearm, waiting 15–20 minutes before applying the blend to the face or body.

As carrier oils represent more than 95 per cent of any massage mix, they should be taken into account when treating skin conditions.

Recommended Carrier Oils

Macadamia
There are several species of macadamia worldwide, of which five are native to Australia. The first Australian native tree to be developed as a food crop, the monounsaturated oil derived from macadamias is known to be the closest oil to our skin's natural sebum. This means absorption is high, moisture loss is low and it is very nourishing for dry and mature skin. Australian macadamias contain no cholesterol, possess antioxidant properties, are remarkably high in vitamins E, B and A, high in protein, calcium and potassium and very low in sodium. Also known as the bobble nut, Queensland nut and by Aboriginals as *kindal kindal*.

Sweet almond
A protein-rich oil of mild aroma that contains vitamins A, B1, B2 and B6 and a small amount of vitamin E. Nourishing for the skin, it has a long shelf-life and blends well with other carrier oils.

Apricot kernel
Often a key ingredient in facial tonics and cosmetics, with similar properties to sweet almond oil. It is great for mature and sensitive skins.

Avocado
A nourishing, rich and heavy oil that is often blended with other cold-pressed oils for increased penetration. Effective for dry and dehydrated skin, the unrefined oil is green in colour and contains vitamins A, B1, B2 and E as well as lecithin. This oil also has a mild sunscreen effect.

Carrot
Rich in betacarotene, vitamins B, C, D, E and essential fatty acids. An anti-inflammatory oil and a useful treatment for burns. Considered to have anti-ageing properties, carrot is often found in skin creams. A strong oil, for facial blends it is best mixed with olive and almond oils.

Coconut
A highly saturated oil, coconut oil remains stable for a long time, making it a useful ingredient in cosmetic preparations. Massaged into the scalp daily, it will cause thin hair to thicken and shine.

Evening Primrose
A good oil for treating dry and mature skin.

Grapeseed
A fine polyunsaturated oil with no odour. Good for body massages as it is not sticky and leaves a satiny coating on the skin.

Hazelnut
Good for slightly oily skins, hazelnut is mildly astringent and penetrates easily. Stimulates circulation and is terrific for muscular problems.

Jojoba
A waxy liquid rather than an oil, its powers of penetration are high and it does not become rancid. Excellent for hair and facial blends.

Olive

A warming, calming oil that penetrates easily and softens the skin. Olive oil is effective for treating rheumatism and some skin disorders.

Rosehip

Harvested from a species of wild rose originally found in Chile, this polyunsaturated oil has been used topically in clinical practice with amazing results. Acne, eczema, dermatitis, cracked, aged and sun-damaged skin, scars, stretch marks, burns, wounds and over-pigmented skin have all been shown to benefit from rosehip oil.

Wheatgerm

A heavy, rich oil, often too greasy to use on its own but helps slow rancidity when blended with other carrier oils. Contains high concentrations of vitamin E.

Mood Makers

Simple yet effective, these essential oil blends can be used in baths, vaporisers and burners, or mixed in massage blends as mood therapy.

Pampering: 3 drops rose, 3 drops neroli, 3 drops lavender.

Reviving: 2 drops lemon, 2 drops peppermint, 2 drops pine, 3 drops rose.

Balancing: 4 drops geranium, 3 drops neroli, 2 drops rose.

Calming: 4 drops Roman chamomile, 4 drops rose.

Euphoric: 3 drops lavender, 2 drops orange, 3 drops clary sage, 2 drops ylang ylang.

Grounding: 3 drops bergamot, 2 drops atlas cedar, 4 drops lavender, 3 drops sandalwood.

Uplifting: 4 drops bergamot, 3 drops clary sage, 4 drops ylang ylang.

Homegrown Favourites

Tea Tree (*Melaleuca alternifolia*)

One of Australia's contributions to the hundreds of essential oils on the market today is the native Australian tea tree. Aboriginals recognised the healing powers of tea tree many thousands of years ago and used it to treat wounds and infections. Captain James Cook used the fragrant leaves in a tea to prevent scurvy among his crew, which is how the name originated. A powerful antiseptic and disinfectant, its "cure-all" effects saw tea tree oil included as standard issue in first-aid kits of the Australian Army and Navy during World War II. In the outback, it was traditionally used as a medicine for coughs and colds.

Tea tree oil can be used to treat a multitude of ailments, from cuts and scratches to fungal infections, insect bites, acne and colds. Mild on the skin, the immune-boosting qualities of tea tree oil protect healthy tissue and defend damaged cells from attack by germs. Uplifting and stimulating, it is also good for post-shock symptoms, depression, low morale and fatigue. Used as an inhalation or dabbed directly onto sores or acne, tea tree is fast-acting and effective.

Eucalyptus (*Eucalyptus* sp)

A dynamic oil of Australian origin, eucalyptus has a cleansing effect on the mind and body. Eucalypts or "gum trees" are a beloved part of the Australian landscape and with over 400 varieties of trees and shrubs, are the most plentiful native tree in the country. Australian Aboriginals called them *kino* and would bind the healing leaves around wounds. In the early days of the colony a concoction called "Sydney peppermint," which contained oil that was extracted from eucalyptus leaves, was exported to England as a digestive tonic.

Eucalyptus brings energy and vitality to any circumstances or situation that seems stagnant.

A powerful general antiseptic, disinfectant and antiviral essential oil, eucalyptus works quickly to clear infection and relieve respiratory disorders, coughs, colds and flu. Fevers, rheumatism and arthritis, melancholy, exhaustion and lack of concentration are also helped by the therapeutic use of eucalyptus oil. A stimulating and activating decongestant that strengthens the immune system and promotes good oxygen uptake by the body, eucalyptus—inhaled or massaged onto the skin—is ideal for people wishing to open up, go with the flow and revitalise.

Eucalyptus has a cooling, refreshing effect on the emotions and helps to clear the head. It is safe for use in compresses, poultices and massage blends, but can be toxic in high doses.

Lemon-scented Myrtle (*Backhousia citriodora*)

A native essential oil used for its enzyme action and refreshing aroma, lemon myrtle is the world's strongest and purest source of citral. It is also an excellent antiseptic and has an aroma of rich, woody lemon. Lemon myrtle is also known to relieve stress and mild anxiety, while stimulating circulation. As their name suggests, lemon-scented myrtle leaves have a lemony fragrance; dried or fresh, they make a wonderfully refreshing tea. When lemon essence was in short supply in World War II, the Australian soft drink company Tarax used lemon-scented myrtle in their lemonade. Now that lemon myrtles are commercially farmed, distilled oils, leaves and seeds are widely available for culinary use, cosmetics and perfumes.

Blue Cypress (*Callitris intratropica*)

Australian blue cypress essential oil represents the earthy, fresh and alive environment of Australia. A grounding oil, blue cypress comes from sustainable plantations of the *Callitris intratropica* tree in the Northern Territory and captures the clean, healthy and active essence of the Australian lifestyle.

Bark resins from the blue cypress have been used for centuries by local indigenous Tiwi people to treat skin lesions and upset stomachs. When distilled the wood produces a rich and redolent essential oil of deep blue colour. Its smell is clean, tangy and refreshing in a subtle woody way, with just a hint of lemon and clove.

The tree is known for its termite resistance and early research suggests its oil may be useful for treating warts and viral infections, as well as offering anti-inflammatory properties.

Australian neroli oil and boronia oil are also produced commercially in Australia.

Australian
Spa Cuisine

Healthy and Delicious Eating— the Australian Way

Australia is recognised internationally for having some of the best quality and variety of fresh produce in the world. The nation's multicultural population has contributed to a blending of cuisines, resulting in a diversity of cooking styles and flavours. Regional specialities abound, due to varying climate, soil and growing conditions.

The trend for longer treatment packages and day visits to spas has made the availability of something fresh and delicious to nibble on a necessity. These days we all know how important a low-fat, balanced diet is for our health, weight and wellbeing.

Fresh seafood, easily caught or bought, is something many Australians take for granted. Seafood makes for great spa food—it is easy to digest, low in kilojoules, high in protein and an excellent source of important minerals such as zinc, iodine, potassium and phosphorus. Vitamin-rich fish eaten a few times a week can help to lower cholesterol and reduce the risk of heart disease. Fish is generally low in fat, especially saturated fat, containing less than 2 per cent on average. The good news is that this small amount of fat comprises mostly of omega-3 essential fatty acids, which have many therapeutic qualities. For example, they help prevent artery-blocking blood clots and reduce levels of triglycerides in the body (both contribute to heart disease and diabetes). They are good for dry skin conditions such as eczema and psoriasis. They also help to prevent arthritis. These fatty acids boost the immune system, and are needed by all major body organs to function normally.

Nutritionists—and your mum—are right: eat your vegetables! Each vegetable contains nearly all of the vital nutrients we need, every vitamin (with the exception of B12), every mineral and every kind of dietary fibre. Reports of the diseases vegetables protect against as well as the miracle nutrients they contain may change, but the general advice remains the same—vegetables are good for you.

The same nutritional advice also applies to fruit—it is a great energy booster, cleanser and helps to maintain a healthy body. Studies show that everyone eats more fresh fruit if it is sliced and offered on a platter or used in a recipe. Pineapple, for example, contains the enzyme bromelain, which breaks down protein. It is believed to assist with sleeping problems, in sinus decongestion, to relieve urinary tract infections and as an anti-inflammatory treatment for arthritis.

Prepared with an awareness of people's desire for health and wellbeing, the recipes in this book are just a sample of the sumptuous fare offered to guests in Australian spas and retreats. Most can be enjoyed in the home with the minimum of fuss. We hope you enjoy the selection.

Chamomile, Soy Milk and Strawberry Smoothie

This smoothie is a nutritious digestive and nervous system tonic. Strawberries are used in Chinese medicine to improve appetite and poor digestion. Also rich in vitamin C and silicon, strawberries strengthen corrective tissue. Chamomile is renowned for its calming qualities and also soothes the digestive system.

Ingredients
1 chamomile tea bag
½ cup (125 ml) boiling water
½ cup (125 ml) unsweetened soy milk or low-fat milk, chilled
6–7 fresh strawberries (about 4 oz/125 g)
2 teaspoons wheatgerm

Method
Steep the tea bag in the boiling water for 10 minutes. Remove the tea bag and let the tea cool.

Combine the tea and the remaining ingredients in a blender and purée until smooth.

makes 1 smoothie
Recipe courtesy of Aurora

Apricot, Orange and Ginger Smoothie

A cleansing smoothie that aids in the reduction of cholesterol levels and has an overall tonic action on the mucous membranes of the body (nasal, gut, lungs, bowels and so on). It contains oat bran, a soluble fibre good for sluggish bowels and for reducing cholesterol; orange, an immune system booster rich in vitamin C and bioflavonoids; and ginger, used for menstrual cramps, vomiting, nausea, bronchitis, morning sickness, aches and spasms. Fresh ginger helps the digestive system break down high protein foods such as meats and beans.

Ingredients
5 dried apricots, diced
¾ cup (180 ml) water
Juice of 1 orange (about ½ cup/125 ml)
2 teaspoons oat bran
1 teaspoon finely grated fresh ginger

Method
In a saucepan, combine the apricots and water and bring to a boil. Reduce the heat, cover and cook for 15 minutes. Cool and combine the liquid and remaining ingredients in a blender. Blend until very smooth.

makes 1 smoothie
Recipe courtesy of Aurora

Nigiri Sushi

Sushi Rice
2 cups (400 g) short-grain Japanese rice
2½ cups (625 ml) water
½ cup (125 ml) mirin (sweet Japanese rice wine)
1½ tablespoons sugar
¼ teaspoon salt

Sushi Toppings
4 fresh shrimp, deveined and slit along the belly
1 tablespoon sake
Salt
Mirin (extra)
Water (extra)
4 slices fresh tuna (about 3 oz/90 g), cut into
    finger-length rectangles
4 slices fresh squid (about 1½ oz/50 g), cut into
    finger-length rectangles
4 slices fresh salmon or ocean trout (about 3 oz/
    90 g), cut into finger-length rectangles
Prepared wasabi paste
Sliced pickled ginger, to garnish
Japanese soy sauce, for dipping

Method
To make the Sushi Rice, cook the rice in a rice cooker or a saucepan, then transfer the rice to a wooden bowl or tray and spread out evenly. Mix the mirin, sugar and salt in a bowl until the sugar and salt are dissolved, and sprinkle the mixture over the rice. Using a wooden spatula, combine the rice and mirin mixture with a cutting motion, using a hand-held or electric fan to evaporate the extra liquid. Cover with a piece of cloth and leave for 3–4 minutes.

To prepare the Sushi Toppings, place the shrimp in a saucepan with enough water to cover. Add the sake and a pinch of salt, and blanch for 30 seconds or until the shrimp just turn pink. Remove from the saucepan and allow the shrimp to cool. Peel the shrimp, leaving the tails intact. Open the shrimp belly lengthways along the pre-cut slit and flatten out.

Wet hands with a mixture of equal parts mirin and water. Scoop up a little rice (enough for 1–2 bites). Place the rice in one palm and cup fingers around it. Form into a rectangular shape by pressing down lightly with the index and middle fingers of your other hand. Smear the underside of the shrimp, fish and squid with a little wasabi paste. Place the rice rectangle on top and press lightly together. Serve with sliced ginger, wasabi and Japanese soy sauce.

serves 4 as an appetizer
Recipe courtesy of Shizuka Ryokan

Pickled ginger is made from thin slices of young, red-coloured ginger pickled in salt and vinegar. It is sold in jars in well-stocked supermarkets.

Japanese soy sauce is saltier than the Chinese variety. Chinese soy sauce makes an acceptable substitute, but a good quality Japanese soy sauce is a must if you intend to cook a lot of Japanese food.

Mirin is a sweet cooking rice wine sold in bottles. If unavailable, use 1 teaspoon sugar dissolved in 2 teaspoons sake.

Wasabi is a pungent root tasting somewhat like a mixture of ginger and hot mustard. It is sold fresh, in powdered form, and as a prepared paste, and can be found in many supermarkets selling Japanese ingredients.

Scallop, Crab and Mango Salad

Ingredients

3 stalks Vietnamese mint (polygonum or *laksa*
   leaves) or any other fresh herbs such as basil
1 stalk coriander leaves (cilantro)
½ head butter lettuce or Boston lettuce
½ head iceberg lettuce or romaine lettuce
1½ cups (about 3½ oz/100 g) baby spinach leaves
1 large mango
1 large finger-length red chilli
3½ oz (100 g) dried rice noodles
24 fresh scallops, shucked (about 8 oz/250 g)
2 teaspoons peanut oil
1 cup (about 4 oz/125 g) cooked crabmeat,
   lightly salted

Dressing

½ inch (1 cm) fresh young ginger, peeled
6 tablespoons mirin (sweet Japanese rice wine)
1 piece rock sugar
2 tablespoons cider vinegar
2 teaspoons peanut oil

Method

To make the Dressing, shave the ginger with a
vegetable peeler. Heat the mirin for a few minutes
to cook off the alcohol. Reduce to a simmer and
stir in the ginger.

Pound the sugar in a mortar and pestle and add to
the ginger and mirin. Add the vinegar and cook for
5 minutes. Remove from the heat and add the oil.

Wash and pluck the mint and coriander (cilantro)
leaves, discarding the stems. Wash the lettuce
leaves and slice finely. Wash the baby spinach
leaves, tearing them into smaller pieces.

Peel and slice the mango into bite-sized pieces.
Blanch the chilli and slice finely. Blanch the rice
noodles and set aside.

Sear the scallops in hot peanut oil until brown on
both sides.

To assemble, place the salad on a serving plate.
Toss all the other ingredients (except the Dressing)
in a bowl. Pile on top of the salad, and—after
shaking—drizzle the Dressing over it.

serves 4 to 6
Recipe courtesy of Azabu/Spice Gourmet Catering

Grilled Swordfish with Herb Dressing

Ingredients

1¼ lbs (600 g) fresh swordfish fillets
1 head romaine lettuce
Salt and pepper
Olive oil, to baste
15 cherry tomatoes, cut in half
15 teardrop tomatoes, cut in half
12 capers, cut in half
Lemon wedges and fresh herbs, to garnish

Herb Dressing

3 cups (about 4 oz/120 g) mixture of fresh herbs
    such as parsley, basil and oregano
2 teaspoons olive oil
Juice of 2 medium lemons
Salt and pepper

Method

To make the Herb Dressing, place the herbs and olive oil in a blender and process until smooth. Add the lemon juice and season with salt and pepper.

Clean the swordfish and cut into individual servings. Pick the romaine lettuce leaves from the hearts. Cut the leaves in half, wash and dry the leaves and hearts thoroughly. Season the lettuce hearts with a dash of salt and pepper, then drizzle a bit of olive oil on the lettuce hearts.

Season the fish and grill for 1 minute on each side on a very hot grill plate with the lettuce hearts.

(Swordfish should not be overcooked as its flesh becomes very dry.)

Sauté both types of tomato and the capers in a little olive oil. To serve, place the romaine hearts on a plate first, then place the fish on top, surrounded by the tomatoes and capers. Drizzle Herb Dressing on the fish and garnish with a lemon wedge.

serves 4
Recipe courtesy of Hyatt Regency Coolum

Salmon and Shrimp Fettuccine with Sweet Thai Chilli Sauce

Ingredients

1 lb (500 g) fresh fettuccine or Chinese egg noodles, or about 8 oz (250 g) dried noodles, boiled according to the instructions on the packet.

12 kaffir lime leaves, 6 sliced as thinly as possible, the rest left whole

3 tablespoons peanut oil

4 fresh salmon fillets (about 7 oz/200 g each), skin and bones removed

12 fresh shrimp (about 5 oz/140 g), peeled and skewered

12–15 pistachios (about 3½ oz/100 g), shelled and roughly chopped

1 spring onion, sliced

Sweet Thai Chilli Sauce

½ cup (100 g) palm sugar or brown sugar

½ bird's eye chilli

3 tablespoons water

Juice of 1 lime

5 tablespoons fish sauce

1½ finger red chillies, deseeded and sliced finely lengthways

½ in (1 cm) fresh young ginger, sliced finely into thin julienned strips

Method

Bring the water to a boil in a medium-sized pot and cook the noodles for 4 minutes. Drain.

Fry the whole kaffir lime leaves in a wok or skillet using 1 tablespoon of the peanut oil for 1 minute until crispy, remove from the plate and set aside.

Sear the salmon in the same oil, for 30 seconds on each side. Place the salmon under a medium grill to crisp.

In the same wok or skillet used for the salmon, cook the shrimp, turning once and removing from the heat before they finish cooking.

Heat the remaining 2 tablespoons of peanut oil in a wok and toss the shredded kaffir lime leaves, pistachios and spring onion until slightly cooked, or for about 2 minutes. Add the noodles and cook until warmed through.

To make the Sweet Thai Chilli Sauce, place the palm sugar, bird's eye chilli and water in a saucepan over medium heat and cook until the sugar has dissolved. Add the lime juice, fish sauce, chilli, ginger and cook for 10–15 minutes until flavours are infused.

To assemble, divide the noodles between 4 plates and top with salmon and shrimp. Drizzle with the Sweet Thai Chilli Sauce, distributing chilli and ginger evenly. Garnish with the whole lime leaves.

serves 4

Recipe courtesy of Azabu/Spice Gourmet Catering

Pan-fried Fish with Polenta and Spinach

This dish is most delicious when cooked with barramundi, one of Australia's best eating fish. Barramundi is found in the brackish rivers, creeks, swamps and streams of lush tropical and subtropical northern Australia. Other firm-fleshed fish like salmon can also be used.

Ingredients
4 cups (1 litre) water
1 cup (200 g) polenta (cornmeal)
1¼ lbs (600 g) barramundi or salmon fillets
8 oz (250 g) baby spinach leaves
Pepper, salt and nutmeg, to taste

Sweet Cucumber Pickles
1 cucumber, thinly sliced across
½ cup (100 g) sugar
1 cup (250 ml) rice wine vinegar

Method
First make the Sweet Cucumber Pickles by mixing the sugar and vinegar together in a small saucepan, add the cucumber and bring to a boil. Turn off the heat, remove the cucumber from the mixture, drain and and allow to cool.

Place the water in a large saucepan and bring to a boil. Stir in the polenta and continue to stir for 5–7 minutes or until the polenta is thick. Pour into a baking dish coated with a bit of olive oil, and refrigerate until firm. Before serving, grill the polenta until golden and cut into 4 serving pieces.

Baste the fish fillets in olive oil, then pan-fry in a hot pan, skin side only, for 5 minutes. Blanch the spinach and season with pepper, salt and a touch of nutmeg.

To serve, place the spinach on a plate and place the fish on top. Add a wedge of polenta and finish with a few slices of the Sweet Cucumber Pickles.

serves 4
Recipe courtesy of Total Living Centre, Couran Cove Resort

Prawn and Vegetable Tempura

Ingredients

4 fresh large shrimp
4 fresh shiitake mushrooms
1 green bell pepper, halved, deseeded and cut into
    2 in (5 cm) pieces
2 small Japanese eggplants, halved lengthways
½ sweet potato, peeled and cut into ¼ in
    (6 mm) slices
Oil for deep-frying

Batter

2 cups (400 g) sifted flour
1½ cups (375 ml) iced water

Dipping Sauce

1 cup (250 ml) dashi stock, made by dissolving
    ½ teaspoon dashi stock granules in 1 cup hot
    water (see note below)
3 tablespoons Japanese soy sauce
3 tablespoons mirin (sweet Japanese rice wine)

Condiments

2 in (5 cm) daikon radish, grated (optional)
2 in (5 cm) fresh young ginger, grated

Method

To make the Batter, briefly fold the flour in a bowl through the water using chopsticks. The mixture should be lumpy and not overly mixed, and it should be kept very cold. Place the bowl in a bed of ice if necessary.

To make the Dipping Sauce, bring all ingredients to a boil in a saucepan, immediately turn off the heat and allow to cool.

Cut the heads off the shrimp, remove the shells but leave the tails on. Devein and make a few cuts along the belly to prevent curling during cooking. Trim the tail tips and press out excess water to prevent splattering during deep-frying. Cut the stems off the shiitake mushrooms and make a crisscross incision on top of each cap.

Heat the oil to 165°–180°C (350°F). Test by dropping in a small drop of batter in it—it should bubble and float to the top. Begin by frying the vegetables first. Dip the vegetables into the batter, slide into the oil, turning once or twice for even cooking. Drain on paper towels. For the shrimp, hold the tail with fingers and dip into the batter, leaving the tail uncoated. Fry until the batter sets.

Serve the tempura with the Dipping Sauce and some daikon and ginger, separately or mixed.

serves 4 as an appetizer
Recipe courtesy of Shizuka Ryokan

Dashi stock granules are available in most Asian supermarkets. To make 1 cup (250 ml) of dashi stock, stir ½ teaspoon granules in 1 cup hot water. The granules contain salt, so you may want to reduce the soy sauce.

Grilled Tuna with Greek Salad

Ingredients

5 oz (150 g) fresh tuna steak
Olive oil, for drizzling
Lemon juice, for drizzling

Greek Salad
6 black olives, pitted
1 small ripe tomato, diced
½ red onion, diced
½ cucumber, diced or sliced
1 tablespoon crumbled low-fat cheese
1 tablespoon olive oil
1 tablespoon lemon juice

Method

To make the Greek Salad, combine all the ingredients and toss to mix well.

Lightly grill the tuna on both sides until cooked to your liking.

Arrange the tuna and salad as desired on a plate, and drizzle with the olive oil and lemon juice.

serves 1
Recipe courtesy of Aurora

Nutritional notes from Aurora's naturopath, Lindy Cook.

Onions *have antioxidant qualities and, in Chinese medicine, are believed to promote warmth and help purify the body. They cleanse arteries, reduce blood pressure, cholesterol, phlegm as well as inflammation of the nose and throat. According to Chinese medicine,* **tomatoes** *are good for the stomach, cleanse the liver and detoxify the body in general.* **Cucumber** *is a cooling vegetable, believed to counteract toxins and lift depression. It also contains a digestive enzyme that can aid the breakdown of proteins and is believed to destroy worms, especially tapeworm.* **Olives** *produce a monounsaturated or "good" fat. Olives are beneficial for dry skin conditions and increase the absorption of fat soluble vitamins A, D, E and K.* **White cheese** *is generally lower in fat than yellow cheese and therefore suitable for low-cholesterol diets and weight-loss programmes.* **Tuna**—*although an oily fish   is low in fat and high in nutritional value.*

Lobster Salad with Melon and Sweet Chilli

Slipper lobsters, also known as Moreton Bay Bugs in Australia, are similar to crayfish and are caught mostly off the eastern coast of Australia. If slipper lobsters are unavailable, you can substitute with fresh tiger prawns or lobsters.

Ingredients

12 watermelon balls
12 cantaloupe balls
12 honeydew melon balls
2½ tablespoons bottled sweet chilli sauce
4 large or 8 small fresh slipper lobsters, or tiger prawns or 2 regular lobsters
Olive oil
7 oz (200 g) arugula (rocket), washed and drained until dry
2 bunches fresh coriander leaves (cilantro), chopped

Method

Marinate the melon balls in the chilli sauce for 2 hours until the juices are well mixed.

Blanch the lobsters in hot, salty water for 8 minutes. Refresh in ice water and cut in half from head to tail. Remove the flesh from the lobsters or prawns and shred if using bigger ones.

To serve, scatter well-drained arugula (rocket) leaves over the plate. Add the lobster meat, making sure there is height in the dish. Add the chopped coriander (cilantro) leaves to the melon mixture. Scoop the melon balls over and around the salad using the chilli and melon juices as your dressing. Arrange them on one side of salad or stand and wedge into salad. Sprinkle with more coriander (cilantro) leaves if desired and serve immediately.

serves 4
Recipe courtesy of Total Living Centre, Couran Cove Resort

Fresh Oysters
in a Tangy Sauce

This dish is served with a spicy Japonnaise Sauce, which is an Oriental version of a Bloody Mary.

Ingredients
1 dozen fresh oysters
½ lemon, sliced in wedges
½ lime, sliced in wedges

Tangy Japonnaise Sauce
1 tablespoon very finely diced celeriac (celery root)
1 tablespoon finely diced carrot
1 tablespoon very finely diced green zucchini skin
1 tablespoon very finely diced red onion
Tomato juice (to bind)
A few drops of Worcestershire sauce, to taste
A few drops of Tabasco sauce, to taste
A few drops of sesame oil
Salt and pepper, to taste

Method
To make the Japonnaise Sauce, combine all the ingredients in a bowl and chill.

To serve, shuck the oysters and place one oyster into each soup spoon and arrange them in a circle on a serving plate. Douse each oyster with the chilled Tangy Japonnaise Sauce. Serve with lemon and lime wedges.

serves 1–2
Recipe courtesy of Dunk Island

Steamed Fish with Salad and Honey Lime Dressing

Spotted cod, nannygai, rosy jobfish and other fresh reef fish found off Australia's East Coast are ideal for this recipe, but any other white-fleshed fish like coral trout or snapper will do just as well. A local avocado blossom honey is used, but may be substituted with ordinary honey if unavailable.

Ingredients

1½ lbs (700 g) fish fillets (skin left on), cut into 4 portions
4 handfuls of arugula (rocket), mesclun or other fresh salad greens
4 handfuls of snowpeas, steamed or blanched
4 handfuls of yellow or red cherry tomatoes, halved
4 wedges papaya, thinly sliced
16 asparagus spears, sliced into quarters, blanched

Honey Lime Dressing
1 cup (250 ml) dry white wine
7 oz (200 g) low-fat butter, chilled and diced
Avocado blossom honey, to taste
Lime juice, to taste
Salt and pepper
½ cup (100 g) finely chopped chives
1 tablespoon flying fish roe (*tobiko*)

Method

To make the Honey Lime Dressing, heat the white wine in a heavy saucepan over low to medium heat, and reduce by half. Gradually add the diced butter, a little at a time, stirring continuously. Be careful not to let the pan get too hot or the sauce will separate. When all the butter has been mixed in, remove from the heat and add honey and lime juice to taste. Season with salt and pepper, add the chives and fish roe and gently stir.

Steam the fish in a bamboo basket over a pot of boiling water until just firm, or for 2–3 minutes. Arrange the salad greens in the centre of a plate and tumble through the snowpeas, tomatoes, papaya and asparagus. Place the hot fish on top, skin side up, and spoon the butter sauce around the salad.

serves 4
Recipe courtesy of Dunk Island

Baked Fish with Herbs, Mushrooms and Vegetables

Ingredients

2 medium potatoes (about 4 oz/120 g each)
½ cup (about 100 g) uncooked brown rice
1 cup (250 ml) water
2 cups (about 7 oz/200 g) button mushrooms
½ clove garlic
Juice of 4 lemons (about 1 cup/250 ml)
½ cup fresh herbs such as parsley, basil and thyme
4 small ripe tomatoes, diced
1¼ lbs (600 g) fresh fish fillets (snapper, sea perch or any firm white fish)
2 teaspoons extra virgin olive oil
6 baby carrots (6 oz/180 g), peeled and sliced, blanched for 1 minute
Lemon wedges and fresh herbs, to garnish

Method

Bake the potatoes in an oven at 200°C (400°F) for about 45 minutes. Cut each in half when done.

Cook the brown rice in the water in a rice cooker or a saucepan.

Steam the mushrooms for 6 minutes. Remove from the steamer and reserve the remaining liquid. Slice the mushrooms thinly and add to the liquid with the garlic, ½ cup (125 ml) lemon juice, the herbs and the diced tomatoes.

Divide the fish into 4 portions and pan-fry in the olive oil for about 1 minute on each side. Place the fish in the oven with the potatoes to finish cooking, about 6–8 minutes, depending on the type of fish used.

To serve, place half a potato, along with a scoop of carrots and a scoop of brown rice on each plate. Place the fish on top, pour over the remaining lemon juice and finish by spooning the mushroom mixture and juices over the dish. Garnish with a lemon wedge and fresh herbs.

serves 4

Recipe courtesy of Hyatt Regency Coolum

Pasta with Fresh Seafood and Tomatoes

Ingredients

2–3 large fresh tomatoes (about 1 lb/450 g), cored
1 clove garlic
1 tablespoon sliced chilli
1 bunch basil, torn
2 teaspoons extra virgin olive oil
8–10 fresh large shrimp (8 oz/250 g), peeled, deveined and cut in half
8–10 fresh shucked scallops (6 oz/170 g) with roe
8 oz (250 g) fillet of snapper, trout, mackerel or any fresh firm white fish
5 oz (150 g) fresh cuttlefish strips
14 oz (450 g) fresh wholemeal pasta
Basil or dill, to garnish

Method

Blanch the tomatoes in boiling water for 10 seconds. Remove and plunge in ice water. Cool, quarter, remove seeds and dice the flesh. Marinate in garlic, chilli, basil and 1 teaspoon olive oil. Chill.

Clean and cut seafood into bite-sized pieces.

Bring a pan of water to a boil and cook the pasta until *al dente*.

While the pasta is cooking, heat a large pan or wok on the stove. Add the remaining olive oil, then add the seafood and pan-fry for several minutes. Add the tomatoes and simmer until the seafood is cooked. Add the pasta and toss through. Season to taste and garnish with herbs.

serves 4
Recipe courtesy of Hyatt Regency Coolum

Chicken with Asparagus and Saffron Risotto

Ingredients

2 small red bell peppers
14 oz (400 g) skinless chicken breast
3 oz (80 g) ricotta cheese (about 4 tablespoons)
Large handful of herbs of your choice, chopped
Salt and pepper, to taste
2 medium onions, diced
1½ tablespoon olive oil
1 cup (200 g) uncooked risotto rice
2 cups (500 ml) vegetable stock
Pinch of saffron
8 fresh asparagus spears, sliced into thirds
1½ cups (150 g) fresh or frozen peas, blanched
5 oz (150 g) fresh or frozen green beans, halved
    and blanched

Method

Roast the red bell peppers in a hot oven or under the broiler until they start to blister, turning to roast evenly on all sides. Remove from the oven, place in a bowl, cover with clingwrap and allow to cool (the steam makes it easier to peel the skins off the peppers).

Remove any fat from the chicken. Divide the chicken into 4 portions and slightly flatten the portions into cutlets.

Mix the ricotta with some herbs and season to taste. Spread the ricotta mixture on the chicken and roll up. Secure the ends with a toothpick and set aside.

Peel the bell peppers, remove the seeds and blend the flesh in a food processor and keep warm.

Sauté the onion in a skillet with 1 tablespoon of the olive oil until soft and translucent, but do not brown. Add the risotto rice, vegetable stock and saffron. Simmer for about 10 minutes on low heat until all the stock is gone and the rice is soft.

In a separate pan, fry the chicken rolls in the remaining olive oil to a light brown colour on all sides. Finish cooking in a hot oven (how long it takes depends on the size of the rolls).

Cut the chicken rolls at an angle with a sharp knife and serve with some risotto, asparagus, peas and beans, and some sauce on the side.

serves 4

Recipe courtesy of Hyatt Regency Coolum

Chicken and Vegetable One-Pot

Ingredients

1 head broccoli (14 oz/400 g), cut into florets
2 carrots, peeled and sliced
3½ oz (100 g) shimeji or shiitake mushroom
1 cake firm tofu (about 8 oz/250 g), sliced
1 lb (500 g) skinless chicken breast, cut into
  bite-sized pieces
7 oz (200 g) dried soba (buckwheat) noodles, boiled
  in water for 3 minutes until soft, drained

Soup

3 cups (1 litre) water
½ teaspoon dashi stock granules, dissolved in 1 cup
  (250 ml) hot water (see page 167)
2 tablespoons Japanese soy sauce
2 tablespoons sake
2 tablespoons mirin

Method

To make the Soup, boil the water in a saucepan.
Reduce to a simmer and add the other ingredients.

Bring to the boil again. Reduce the heat to medium
and add the chicken. Simmer for 10 minutes. In
the meantime, cook the vegetables in a large pot or
steamer until soft. Divide the cooked ingredients
and noodles into 4 individual serving bowls. Pour
in the soup, cover for 5 minutes and serve.

serves 4
Recipe courtesy of Shizuka Ryokan

Miso Soup with Tofu

Ingredients

1½ teaspoons dashi stock granules
  dissolved in 3 cups (750 ml) hot water
1 teaspoon miso
1 small cake tofu (about 5 oz/150 g), diced
1 spring onion, minced
1 tablespoon wakame (dried seaweed,
  available in Asian supermarkets)

Method

Heat the dashi stock until boiling. Reduce
the heat to very low, and add the miso.
Miso soup should never boil so remove from heat
if serving at once or lower to a gentle simmer.
Place the tofu, a sprinkling of spring onion and
wakame in 4 individual soup bowls, pour over the
soup, and serve immediately.

serves 4
Recipe courtesy of Shizuka Ryokan

Chicken with Wild Rice Pilaf

Ingredients

2 medium red bell peppers

½ teaspoon cracked pepper

4 skinless chicken breasts, fat removed

8 baby onions, peeled and sliced

1 clove garlic, bruised and left whole

2½ tablespoons tomato juice

1 medium carrot, peeled and sliced
    thinly into strips lengthwise

1 medium zucchini, sliced thinly into
    strips lengthwise

16 green beans

Wild Rice Pilaf

1 medium onion, finely diced

1 clove garlic, chopped

½ cup (100 g) uncooked wild rice

½ cup (100 g) uncooked long-grain rice

2 cups (500 ml) vegetable stock

1 bay leaf

2 sprigs fresh thyme

Salt and pepper, to taste

Method

To make the Wild Rice Pilaf, place the onion and garlic in a non-stick heat-proof skillet over moderate heat and sweat until transparent. Pour in the rices and mix through. Add the vegetable stock, bay leaf and half the thyme. Stir frequently, and heat until simmering. Cover with a lid heat at 170°C (325°F) for 15 minutes until cooked. Remove from the oven and break up the mixture with a fork. Season with salt and pepper. Keep warm.

Sear the bell peppers in a non-stick pan over high heat to blister the skin on all sides, then place in a hot oven (220°C/425°F) for 20 minutes to cook through until soft. Remove and place in a bowl, cover with clingfilm and set aside to cool. When the peppers have cooled, peel and chop the flesh into chunks, then place in a food processor and blend until smooth. Season with the cracked pepper.

Place the chicken breasts and baby onions in a non-stick pan over moderate heat. Cook until both sides of the chicken and onions are light golden brown. Rub the garlic clove over the chicken and sprinkle with the thyme. Place in an oven preheated to 185°C (350°F) for 15–20 minutes until just cooked. Remove the chicken and allow to rest in a warm place. Return the onions to the oven and bake to a rich golden brown. Set aside.

Cook the vegetables for 5–6 minutes in a steamer. To serve, heat the bell pepper purée and add some tomato juice to keep it at a sauce consistency. Place the Wild Rice Pilaf on 4 serving plates, slice the chicken and arrange over the rice, then arrange the vegetables, spooning the sauce around the chicken.

serves 4
Recipe courtesy of Daintree Eco Lodge

Grilled Tofu Teriyaki

Ingredients

2 large or 4 small cakes firm tofu
    (about 1¼ lbs/600 g total), sliced
4 cups (400 g) mesclun
2 carrots, julienned
2 leeks, julienned
2 red bell peppers, deseeded and julienned

Coriander and Mint Dressing
12–15 coriander leaves (cilantro)
12–15 mint leaves
3 tablespoons extra virgin olive oil
1½ tablespoons white wine vinegar

Teriyaki Marinade
1 cup (250 ml) bottled teriyaki sauce
1½ tablespoons brown sugar
Handful of chopped coriander leaves (cilantro)
Handful of chopped mint leaves

Method

Make the Coriander and Mint Dressing by blending all the ingredients in a food processor.

Make the Teriyaki Marinade by combining the ingredients in a bowl, stirring until the sugar dissolves. Marinate the tofu for 30 minutes.

Broil or barbecue the tofu until warmed through and golden brown on the outside. Mix well with the salad. Arrange on a serving plate, splash with the Coriander and Mint Dressing and serve.

serves 4

Recipe courtesy of The Dome Retreat/Brisbane Marriott

Zucchini Risotto

Creamy yet resilient to the bite and with big flavours, risotto makes a fulfilling and comforting one-dish meal.

Ingredients
3 medium or 2 large zucchini
1 cup (250 ml) vegetable or chicken stock

Risotto
1 small onion, diced

2 cloves garlic, minced
2 tablespoons olive oil
2 cups (400 g) uncooked risotto rice
½ cup (125 ml) white wine
8 cups (2 litres) hot vegetable or chicken stock
Salt and pepper, to taste
Freshly grated parmesan

Method
Make the Risotto by first cooking the onion and minced garlic gently in a large skillet in the olive oil until soft and translucent, about 2 minutes. Add the rice to the onions and continue frying, stirring constantly, for another 2 minutes. Then add the wine and enough hot stock to just cover the rice. Bring the stock to a boil and stir well. Continue adding the stock in small amounts until the rice is almost cooked.

While the rice is cooking, peel the zucchini and reserve the skins. Bring the stock to a boil in a saucepan. Place the skins in the liquid for 1 minute. Remove from the pot and purée the skins and stock in a blender. Dice the peeled zucchini flesh.

When the rice is almost cooked add the zucchini purée and mix well. Add the diced zucchini. Season with salt and pepper and sprinkle with cheese. Serve hot.

serves 4
Recipe courtesy of Park Hyatt, Melbourne

Gazpacho

Ingredients

¼ loaf crusty sourdough bread (1 day old)
½ red onion, diced
1–2 stalks celery (about 4 oz/125 g), diced
½ clove garlic
½ cucumber, peeled and deseeded
3 ripe tomatoes, diced
½ red bell pepper, deseeded and diced
6 cups (1½ litres) tomato juice
¾ cup (175 ml) olive oil
1–2 tablespoons sherry or balsamic vinegar
Salt and pepper, to taste
Minced fresh chives or herbs of choice, to garnish

Method

Remove the crusts from the bread and cut it into squares. Soften with water. Place the vegetables in a food processor, add half the tomato juice and blend to form a fine purée. Add the softened bread to the vegetable purée, then the olive oil, the rest of the tomato juice and the sherry vinegar to taste. Blend until well mixed and pass through a fine strainer. Season with salt and pepper. Chill well.

Serve the soup in bowls, garnished with fresh herbs, with more bread, if desired.

serves 4–6
Recipe courtesy of Park Hyatt, Melbourne

Pavlova with Fresh Summer Berries

The pavlova, popularly known as a New Zealand creation, actually originated from Australia. This sweet was whipped up in the kitchen of Hotel Esplanade, Perth, to commemorate the visit of the famous Russian ballerina, Anna Pavlova, and was subsequently named after her.

Ingredients
4 egg whites, room temperature
2 teaspoons vanilla extract
Seeds of 1 vanilla pod
½ cup (3½ oz/100 g) superfine castor sugar
12 fresh strawberries (about 8 oz/250 g)
2 cups (400 g) fresh raspberries, frozen
2½ cups (500 g) fresh blueberries
2 cups (400 g) fresh blackberries
8 oz (250 g) low-fat ricotta cheese, beaten with
 a little honey (if too thick add some low-fat
 plain yoghurt)

Raspberry Coulis
2 cups (500 ml) water
Zest of 1 lemon
1½ cups (11 oz/300 g) sugar
1 lb (500 g) frozen raspberries

Method
To make the Raspberry Coulis, bring the water, lemon zest and sugar to a boil in a saucepan, then lower the heat and simmer for 10 minutes.

Place the frozen raspberries in a bowl and pour the hot syrup over. Purée the mixture with a hand mixer, then pass the purée through a fine strainer to remove all the seeds. Set aside and allow to cool.

Place the egg whites in a mixing bowl with the vanilla extract and vanilla seeds. Whisk the egg whites to soft peaks with a mixer, then slowly add the sugar, beating to form a meringue. When the mixture is ready it should be smooth and glossy. Using a large kitchen spoon, spoon four piles of the mixture onto baking trays. Bake in a preheated oven at 180°C (350°F) for 1 hour or until golden brown. Turn off the oven and leave the pavlova to dry so it crisps on the outside and remains soft and marshmallowy on the inside.

Wash and mix the fresh berries together, being careful not to damage them.

To serve, place the pavlovas on individual plates, then spoon 2 tablespoons of the ricotta on top of each, scatter with the mixed berries and drizzle with the Raspberry Coulis. Dust with icing sugar if desired.

serves 4
Recipe courtesy of Park Hyatt, Melbourne

Passionfruit Jelly with Fresh Berries and Honeydew Sorbet

Ingredients
Extra fresh berries (garnish)

Jelly
12 fresh passionfruits
1 tablespoon superfine castor sugar
1¼ cups (300 ml) water
1 packet agar-agar (1 oz/30 g)

Coulis
½ cup (125 ml) water
1 tablespoon sugar
1 tablespoon honey
1 basket each of blackberries, raspberries
    and blueberries

Sorbet
2 ripe honeydew melons, peeled, seeded and cubed
1¼ cups (300 ml) water
1½ cups (300 g) superfine castor sugar
2 egg whites

Method
To make the Jelly, remove the passionfruit pulp from the skins, strain the flesh into a mixing bowl and discard the seeds. Dissolve the sugar in the water, add the agar-agar and stir until dissolved. Strain the mixture into the passionfruit pulp, discarding any undissolved agar-agar. Set in a rectangular cake pan about ½–¾ in (1–2 cm) deep.

To make the Coulis, heat the water, sugar and honey in a saucepan, stirring to dissolve the sugar. Add the blueberries, remove from the heat and cool. Blend, leaving small bits of blueberry.

To make the Sorbet, purée the melon. Heat the water in a saucepan, add 1 cup (7 oz/200 g) of the sugar and dissolve. Blend the melon purée with the sugar syrup. Churn in an ice-cream machine following the manufacturer's instructions. Just before the sorbet sets, beat the remaining sugar into the egg whites until fluffy and add to the sorbet mixture.

To serve, cut the Jelly diagonally into triangles. Place two triangles on each plate, with a handful of berries, a spoonful of the Coulis and a scoop of the Sorbet on the side.

serves 6

Recipe courtesy of Azabu/Spice Gourmet Catering

Jelly and sorbet textures vary depending on fruit moisture levels and the amount made. Test the jelly by setting a small amount first. Adjust accordingly.

Native Australian Healing Ingredients

Aniseed myrtle

Aniseed myrtle has been shown to be highly antifungal and antibacterial, with an incredible aroma that is invigorating and clearing. The leaves are often crushed to release the oils.

Bunya bunya nuts (*Araucaria bidwillii*)

The bunya pine grows to 45 metres (148 feet), and is found mainly in the Bunya Bunya mountains in Queensland. Bunya seeds or nuts are produced in large cones, each containing about 70 seeds, encased in a plywood-like shell. The bunya nut is very high in nutrients and protein, is a good source of carbohydrate and oils, and contains many trace elements.

Eucalyptus (*Eucalyptus* sp)

A powerful antiseptic, eucalyptus also has a refreshing and an uplifting aroma. Eucalyptus oil is an anti-inflammatory, antibiotic, diuretic, analgesic and deodoriser with antiviral, stimulating and grounding qualities.

Gum honey

A powerful antiseptic, honey is nourishing to the skin and is known to kill bacteria and speed the process of healing.

Lemon myrtle (*Backhousia citriodora*)

Lemon myrtle is the world's strongest and purest source of citral, a citric acid. An extremely powerful natural antiseptic, it works well with problem skin. It also helps to relieve symptoms of stress and anxiety. Lemon myrtle has antibacterial and antiviral properties and is used to treat respiratory, immune and hormonal functions.

Lilly pilly (*Syzygium australe*)

Lilly pillies are the small pink fruit of rainforest trees found in Eastern Australia. They possess fairly astringent properties and are high in vitamin C and fruit acids beneficial to the skin. The berries' astringent properties make them a good cleanser, while the vitamin C and fruit acids assist in the regeneration and protection of skin cells.

Macadamias (*Macadamia integrifolia*)

Known to Aborigines as the "bopple nut," macadamia nut kernels contain up to 80 per cent oil, an oil known to be similar to the skin's natural sebum. This means ready absorption into the skin and minimal loss of moisture. Macadamias contain predominantly mono-unsaturated oils and have no cholesterol, making them very nourishing for all skin types, especially dry skin. Australian macadamias are high in vitamins E and A, and are a good source of protein, calcium, potassium and are low in sodium.

Muntries (*Kunzea pomifera*)

Also referred to as "munthari," these berries are found in the coastal regions of South Australia and western Victoria. They look like tiny apples, and are rich in nutrients, essential minerals, vitamins and fruit acids. Their high wax content helps nutrients to penetrate deep into the skin and provides continual nourishment by creating a natural barrier against daily abrasives.

Pepper berries

Native pepper berries are incredibly stimulating as well as warming, with strong antimicrobial and antifungal properties. They are mainly used in foot products.

Quandongs (*Santalum acuminatum*)

Also known as the "desert peach," quandongs have a higher vitamin C content than oranges and can be eaten raw. The red quandong kernel is 70 per cent oil and is a rich source of protein.

Riberries
(*Syzygium luehmanii*)

Found in the coastal regions of New South Wales, riberries are rich in essential nutrients as well as minerals, and contain traces of vitamin C, an antioxidant that helps to stimulate new cell growth. The berries also impart fruit acids known to be beneficial to the skin's rejuvenation.

Tasmanian kelp

Drawn from the waters of Bass Strait in Australia, kelp is naturally revitalising to the skin. It contains essential substances such as vitamins A, B-complex, C and E; calcium; sulphur; iodine; iron; niacin; choline; carotene; alginic acid and amino acids. Kelp contains other trace minerals vital for human health, including zinc, boron, chromium, selenium and tin. Certain types of algae have been found to possess molecules that are similar to those in collagen, the substance that gives skin its elasticity and firmness.

Wattleseed
(*Acacia* sp)

Wattleseed are comprised of 32 per cent fibre, 26 per cent carbohydrate, 23 per cent protein and 9 per cent fat. They are rich in monounsaturated fatty acids and polyunsaturated oils.

Wild limes
(*Eremocitrus glauca*)

Very high in vitamin C, tiny wild limes have powerful anti-oxidant qualities and assist in the production of collagen and elastin, stimulating new cell growth.

Wild rosella
(*Hibiscus sabdariffa*)

Wild rosella comes from a bright crimson flower (a member of the hibiscus family) which grows on a medium-to-large shrub found in the coastal and rainforest regions of Northern Australia. The flower exudes a sweet, crisp fragrance, and is known for its high levels of protein. It is also reputed to be a muscle relaxant.

Homegrown Spa Products

All these products are natural, chemical free and not tested on animals. Most are available from department stores and speciality shops in Australia and overseas. For stockists, see the directory at the back of the book.

Air Spa

Formed by Janie Dallas-Kelly, a Sydney naturopath and doctor of traditional Chinese medicine, Air Spa is a small company with a fresh, plant based range of skin and body care products. As a young girl Janie made homeopathic remedies with her grandmother. She now has over 20 years' experience in a wide range of disciplines including herbology, acupressure as well as iridology and has formulated her range using fresh organic botanicals and age-old alchemy lore, combining active ingredients with naturopathic wisdom.

Air Spa's preservative-free products have a lifespan of six weeks from the time they are opened. Consequently, Kelly advises keeping them in the fridge. Designed to protect skin against Australia's aggressive environmental conditions, Kelly believes her aromatic products also accelerate cell renewal, improve skin tone and rejuvenate the skin. Working on the lipidic barrier to stop moisture from escaping, Air Spa products maintain the skin's acid mantle and pH balance. Choose from body and feet soaks, rubs, cremes, mists and oils; facial moisturisers, masks, cleansers and toners; treatment gels for soothing, slimming, firming and exfoliating; and many pure essential oils. Another ingenious creation of Kelly's is a light-weight, perspex foot file perfect for use on calloused skin. The file's replaceable sandpaper screen, rubbed gently over dry and cracked areas, effectively removes dead skin cells on feet, hands and elbows.

Australian Bush Flower Essences

With a herbalist father, grandmother, great-grandmother and great-great-grandmother, it is hardly surprising that Ian White inherited the family's talent for harnessing the healing power of the Australian bush. White spent much time as a boy bushwalking with his grandmother, helping her gather and prepare herbal extracts and tinctures and gaining a complex knowledge of Australia's native flowering plants. A practitioner and teacher of naturopathy, kinesiology and herbal medicine, White has developed a range of over 60 specific flower essences that promote harmony, health as well as general wellbeing.

Along with Brazil, Australia is regarded as having the greatest number of flowering plants in the world. Using the healing properties of flower essences is an ancient art; in Australia they were first recognised by Aboriginals, who would eat a whole flower to obtain its beneficial effects.

Flower essences are powerful catalysts. Prescribed throughout the world by healers, Australian bush flower essences are incorporated into many Australian spa treatments. The effect of the essences is similar to that of meditation, as they bring clarity to the unconscious mind, resolve negative beliefs and directly affect us at the level where we make decisions about our emotions, health, vitality and our relationships. Flower essences also unlock inherent positive qualities such as love, courage and joy. They can be used in a variety of forms and combine easily with all other healing modalities. There are essence drops, mists and creams available individually or in combination, and they can be incorporated with aromatherapy and added to massage oils and oil burners.

In Essence

Originally the brainchild of aroma-therapist Judith White, In Essence began

selling essential oils in Australia in 1986 when aromatherapy was still considered the domain of alternative and new age lifestyles. Now recognised as the leading Aromatherapy company in the country, delivering the purest oils available for their therapeutic efficacy, In Essence specialises in formulating products which offer creative ways to incorporate aromatherapy into every lifestyle. The heart of the range comprises of 40 pure essential oils. These same oils form the basis of all In Essence products, including the pre-blended lifestyle blends and luxurious body care range. A large variety of accessories have also been designed to facilitate the use of essential oils, while massage base oils complement the range.

Jurlique

Jurlique began with the dream of its founders, Dr Jurgen and Ulrike Klein, to produce a pure and natural skincare range using the life force of plants and herbs. Jurgen Klein, a naturopath, chemist and alchemist and his horticulturist and botanist wife Ulrike, emigrated to Australia from Germany with their four children in 1983. The family settled at Mt Barker in the Adelaide Hills and the couple established the first of their biodynamic herb and flower farms and purchased a factory site.

Jurlique provides an extensive range of products for internal and external body care and also operates about 30 Wellness Sanctuary Day Spas and Concept Spa Stores in Australia and overseas. On its two herb farms, the company uses organic biodynamic soil care and no artificial

fertilisers, herbicides or insecticides. Planting, weeding and picking are done by hand, and herbs and flowers are carefully dried and stored before their oils are extracted.

Jurlique's extensive range includes face, body, bath, shower and hair care products, speciality creams like calendula, aroma-therapy essential oils and herbal teas and medicines. Rich in natural antioxidants to strengthen and nurture the skin and delay visible signs of ageing, Jurlique products are made without the use of chemicals, artificial colours or fragrances. Hypo-allergenic and pH-balanced, they are suitable for all skin types, promoting healthy, radiant skin, whatever the age or climate.

OP Therapy

The base ingredients for OP Therapy's beautiful hydrotherapy and hydrating products are sea salt and emu oil. There is a good reason for this. OP Therapy results from the merging of two family run Australian companies, Olsson Industries (which markets emu oil) and Pacific Salt (which harvests macrobiotic sea salt from the Great Barrier Reef). The creation of OP Therapy is the work of Alexandra Olsson, whose passion for natural health care was fostered by her family's interest in alternative and natural therapies.

Alexandra saw an opportunity to create face and body products combining the main elements of each company; a purifying and relaxing range based on sea salt and aromatherapy, and a healing, nourishing and regenerative range based on emu oil and herbal plant extracts.

For centuries, Australian Aborigines have used emu oil for its protective, restorative and softening qualities. Recognised for its amazing healing and anti-inflammatory qualities, research also suggests that emu oil contains remarkable moisturising properties, is able to penetrate the epidermis and possibly reverse the ravages of ageing. The stylishly packaged products include a "Foot Bliss" marble spa, complete with a bag of marbles to massage your feet and the sensual "Bathe Like A Diva," combining rose petals, whole milk, sea salt and essential oils.

Li'Tya

Li'Tya (pronounced "l-dee-a") is an indigenous Australian word meaning "of the Earth." The Li'Tya range of nourishing, cleansing, protecting and pampering spa products taps into the naturally powerful qualities of the Australian environment. Founder Gayle Heron uses ancient knowledge held by the indigenous peoples of Australia and the potent Australian flora, earth, sea minerals and plants of the highest quality and purity.

Li'Tya spa products combine ancient indigenous medicine with aromatherapy, colour therapy and herbalist principles. Heron's body care range is called Baiame. The name Baiame (pronounced "miami" with a "b") is drawn from the Ya-idt-mid-ung tribe of Southeastern Australia and is the name of a creator spirit. Within Baiame is an "aspect of kindness and care for others" that Heron seeks to embody and emulate. She has permission from tribal elders to use the names, in the spirit of sharing Australia's natural wealth with all Australians.

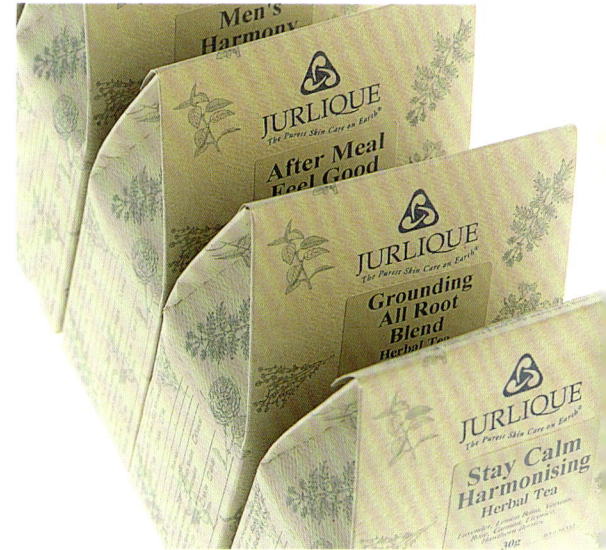

The Li'Tya spa range includes face and body cleansers, toners, herbal, clay and mud masks, hydrating treatments, exfoliants, polishes, body wraps and eye and foot treatments. A percentage of company profits goes to the Baiame Foundation, a non-profit organisation that assists indigenous peoples and projects.

MV Organic Skincare and MV Radiance Treatment Centre

Beyond the merely "natural" products so prevalent on the market today, MV Organic Skincare bridges the gap between beauty therapy and complimentary medicine. The Australian-made range was developed by Sharon McGlinchey, a beauty therapist who recognised a growing need for a sophisticated range of organic and essential oil-based products that would treat clients holistically. Suitable for all skin types, particularly extra-sensitive skins, MV products are formulated using the highest quality essential oils, vegetable oils and plant extracts, and utilises organic ingredients wherever possible. MV feels beautiful, smells great and is free of mineral oil, propylene glycol, parabens, DEA's lanolin, artificial colours and fragrances. No aspect of the product formulation has been compromised for commercial reasons and as a result it is a highly concentrated and pure essential oil product with all the refinement of luxury skincare.

A woman of many talents, Sharon has also combined her extensive experience in beauty therapy with a background in yoga, meditation, Reiki and energy balancing to create a totally new skin and body healing experience. Much more than a beauty salon, MV Radiance is devoted to the idea that good skin results when the mind, body and spirit are in balance. All its customised treatments are designed to improve your total health and wellbeing—as well as maintaining a more youthful, healthy skin.

Purity

Based at Byron Bay in northern NSW, Purity Australia produces a range of skincare and innovative natural products from essential oils to soaps and cosmetic oils. Famous for its sustainable tea tree-growing property, Jenbrook, which is the world's largest producer of standard, organically certified tea tree oil, the company also markets Australian red clay. Obtained from an underground quarry in the Ballarat region of Victoria, this versatile kaolin clay is fine enough to be used daily as a facial scrub, yet efficiently polishes and exfoliates skin, leaving it noticeably smoother.

The Purity team use the clay in their exfoliating masks and hand, foot and body scrubs. They also supply the dry sterilised clay in retail and bulk sizes. Aromatherapy-based water-soluble mask additives are available, enabling one to make specific formulations suited to individual skin types. To make a mask, blend the clay with floral water and the correct mask additive. In Purity's own exfoliating scrub the clay is blended with a range of anti-inflammatory herbal extracts and essential oils of rose and alpine lavender.

Sodashi

Named after an ancient Sanskrit word which means "wholeness, purity and radiance," this is a product range driven by a noble mission; to promote higher levels of consciousness and peace in the world by providing a 100 per cent natural skincare range that provides inner peace and contentment while enhancing the physical, emotional and spiritual well-being of clients.

Sodashi was born of the desire to create products that are 100 per cent natural and unrefined, without animal products or chemicals. Founded by New Zealand-born health and beauty therapist Megan Larsen, Sodashi's goal is to create exquisite therapies for the face and body that are effective and nourishing to the mind, body and spirit.

An Australian skincare range that uses nature's intelligence to nurture the skin, Sodashi has spent many years researching and testing the role that plant essences, also known as "essential oils," play in protecting and nourishing our skin. The result is a divine range of fragrant products that really work. In addition to a comprehensive range of face and body products, there is a men's range and products for use by spa professionals. The delicate but potent essences used by Sodashi are recommended by the world's leading aromatherapists to be the finest possible nourishment for your skin.

PURITY
AUSTRALIA
Australian Red Clay
Base for facial masks
net 100 g

Simple Guide to Spa Etiquette

To help you get the most from your spa experience, The Dome Retreat answers some of the questions their guests most frequently ask.

When should I arrive for my spa treatment?

We suggest you arrive at least 15 minutes before your appointment. This allows ample time to check-in, change, enjoy a herbal tea or water; fill in your treatment card and relax.

What should I wear to the spa?
Wear whatever is comfortable. Spas will provide a robe, slippers and locker for your personal belongings. For any health or healing services, please wear loose, comfortable clothing. If you are participating in any fitness programmes, bring stable athletic shoes. Please bring your swimwear for hydrotherapy or if you would like to relax by the pool or use the spa and sauna.

May I request a male or female therapist?
Definitely. Whether you choose a person of the same or opposite sex, therapists throughout the industry are trained to drape towels and ensure your comfort and privacy at all times.

What do I wear during my treatments?
Our primary concern is your total relaxation. Feel free to enjoy your treatment without clothing, wear your own underwear or our disposable underwear. While some spas request that swimming attire (bottoms) be worn for the Vichy shower and the hydrotherapy spa bath, others may not.

Is there someone to help me decide on the best treatments?

Spa coordinators or a guest relation's coordinator can help you plan your day, or a few precious hours, to suit your needs and interests. The Dome Retreat, along with many other spas, offers a lifestyle consultation to support you on a path to health and wellbeing. By discussing and analysing your needs we can help determine which treatments and programmes will be most beneficial for you.

What if I have special health considerations?
To ensure your maximum safety and comfort a brief personal health history questionnaire is required. We encourage you to disclose any pertinent health conditions that may affect your experience. If you are suffering general health issues such as sinus or headache, we can recommend particular treatments to alleviate your symptoms.

What if I'm late for my appointment?
Arriving late will unfortunately limit the time for your treatment, reducing its effectiveness and your pleasure. Plan your special timeout and ensure you arrive on time to experience the total benefits and pleasure of pampering. All treatments are completed as scheduled.

Why are you so strict with your bookings and cancellations?

We operate The Dome Retreat to the very highest of standards, using the very best products and diligently maintaining environmentally friendly and hygienic day spa practices. We employ more than 25 qualified and highly trained staff and are committed to delivering the ultimate in personal care and service. To ensure the best practice is maintained, we apply the same due diligence to our business affairs.

Can I come earlier or stay later to enjoy the added facilities?

To enhance your journey to relaxation we recommend you come earlier and use the pool, sauna, steam room and spa, or stay after your treatments if this is more convenient. A day at The Dome Retreat can seem like a holiday and the perfect way to rejuvenate so bring your favourite book, a hat and be prepared to indulge in a day of decadence.

What if I'm feeling hungry?

Many spas have their own unique menu of divinely delicious but very healthy and cleansing spa cuisine. Light, tasty and nutritious spa cuisine is incorporated in several Dome Retreat pampering packages, or you may choose to indulge prior to, or following your treatments. As we are a health retreat we serve water or herbal tea with meals and do not have alcohol on our menu.

Spa ambience

The spa environment is one of tranquility and relaxation. Please understand and respect the quiet and privacy needs of other spa guests by lowering your voice and turning off your mobile phone. Enjoy the luxury of silence.

What if I need to cancel my spa appointment?

Out of consideration for all our guests a minimum of 24 hours' notice is required to cancel or reschedule any spa appointment. After that, you will be charged a 50 per cent cancellation fee. No show appointments are charged at full price. Most spas have similar cancellation conditions.

Australian Spa Directory

All information is correct at the time of going to press, but we recommend you call and check before leaving home —businesses may change addresses or names.

Spas

Queensland

The Dome Retreat
Level 4, Brisbane Marriott Hotel
515 Queen Street, Brisbane
Queensland 4000
Tel: + 61 7 3303 8050
Fax: + 61 7 3303 8051
Email: enquiries
@thedomeretreat.com
www.thedomeretreat.com

Daintree Eco Lodge and Spa
20 Daintree Road, Daintree
Queensland 4873
Tel: + 61 7 4098 6100
www.daintree-ecolodge.com.au

Espa
The Sebel Reef House & Spa
99 Williams Esplanade, Palm Cove
Queensland 4879
Tel: + 61 7 4055 3633
Fax: + 61 7 4055 3305
Email: info@reefhouse.com.au
www.reefhouse.com.au

Healing Waters Spa
Silky Oaks Lodge
Finlayvale Road, Mossman
Queensland
Tel: + 61 2 8296 8010
Toll-free: 1300 134044
Email: travel@voyages.com.au
www.voyages.com.au

The Spa of Peace and Plenty
Dunk Island Resort
Tel: + 61 2 8296 8010
Toll-free: 1300 134044
Email: travel@voyages.com.au
www.voyages.com.au

The Sun Spa
Hyatt Regency Coolum
PO Box 78
Warran Road, Coolum Beach
Queensland 4573
Tel: + 61 7 5446 1234
Fax: + 61 7 5446 2957
Email: coolum@hyatt.com.au
www.coolum.hyatt.com

The Spa & Total Living Centre
Couran Cove Island Resort
PO Box 224, Runaway Bay
Queensland 4216
Tel: + 61 7 5597 9997
Toll-free: 1800 268726
Fax: + 61 7 5597 9998
Email: enquiry@couran.com
www.couran.com

Paradise Spa & Bath House
The Towers of Chevron Renaissance
B1/3250 Surfers Paradise Boulevard
Surfers Paradise 4217 Queensland
Tel: + 61 7 5570 6661
Fax: + 61 7 5570 6911
Email: info@paradisespa.com.au
www.paradisespa.com.au

New South Wales

Azabu
317 Skinners Shoot Road
Byron Bay NSW 2481
Tel: + 61 2 6680 9102
Fax: + 61 2 6680 9103
Email: info@azabu.com.au
www.azabu.com.au

Spa Chakra
4/6 Cowper Wharf Road
Woolloomooloo NSW 2011
Tel: + 61 2 9368 0888
Email: spachakra@chakra.net
www.spachakra.com

The Golden Door Health
Retreat—Elysia
Thompsons Road, Pokolbin
NSW 2320
Tel: + 61 2 4993 8500
Toll-free: 1800 212 011
Fax: + 61 2 4993 8599
Email: info@elysia.com.au
www.goldendoor.com.au

Gillian Adams Salon and Spa
1356 Pacific Highway
Turramurra Sydney NSW 2074
Tel: + 61 2 9488 9944
Fax: + 61 2 9488 7961
www.gillianadams.com.au

Lilianfels Blue Mountains Resort
and Spa
Lilianfels Avenue, Echo Point
Katoomba NSW 2780
Tel: + 61 2 4780 1200
Fax: + 61 2 4780 1300
Email: reservations@lilianfels.com.au
www.lilianfels.com.au

The Spa and Fitness Centre
Four Seasons Hotel
199 George Street
Sydney NSW 2000
Tel: + 61 2 9250 3388
Fax: + 61 2 9250 3284
Email: spa.sydney@fourseasons.com
www.fourseasons.com

Victoria

Aurora Spa Retreat
2 Acland Street
St Kilda VIC 3182
Tel: + 61 3 9536 1130
Fax: + 61 3 9525 3729
Email: info@aurorasparetreat.com
www.aurorasparetreat.com

Breathtaker On High
Breathtaker All Suite Hotel and
Alpine Spa Retreat
8 Breathtaker Road, Mt Buller
VIC 3723
Tel: + 61 3 5777 6377
Toll-free: 1800 088 222
Fax: + 61 3 5777 6312
www.breathtaker.com.au

Crown Spa
Crown Towers
Level 3, No. 8 Whiteman Street
Southbank VIC 3006
Tel: + 61 3 9292 6182
www.crowntowers.com.au

Lyall Spa
Ground floor, The Lyall Hotel
14 Murphy Street, South Yarra
Melbourne VIC 3141
Tel: + 61 3 9868 8333
Email: spa@thelyall.com
www.thelyall.com

Natskin Spa Retreat
Immerse Vineyard
1548 Melba Highway
Dixons Creek Yarra Valley VIC 3775
Tel: + 61 3 5965 2500
Email: immerse@natskin.com
www.natskin.com

Park Club Health and Day Spa
Park Hyatt Melbourne
1 Parliament Square
Melbourne VIC 3002
Tel: + 61 3 9224 1222
Fax: + 61 3 9224 1208
Email: phmelbourne@hyatt.com.au
www.melbourne.park.hyatt.com

Salus Spa at the Lake House
Lake House Restaurant and Small
Luxury Hotel
King Street, Daylesford VIC 3460
Tel: + 61 3 5348 3329
Fax: + 61 3 5348 3995
www.lakehouse.com.au

The Spa
The Mansion Hotel
Werribee Park
K Road, Werribee VIC 3030
Tel: + 61 3 9731 4140
Fax: + 61 3 9731 4001
Email: spa@mansiongroup.com.au
www.mansionhotel.com.au

Tasmania

Waldheim Alpine Spa
Cradle Mountain Lodge
Tasmania
Tel: + 61 2 8296 8010
Toll-free: 1300 134044
Email: spa@cradlemountainlodge.com
www.cradlemountainlodge.com.au

Western Australia

Empire Retreat
Caves Road, Yallingup
Western Australia 6282
Tel: + 61 8 9755 2065
Fax: + 61 8 9755 2297
Email: luxury@empireretreat.com
www.empireretreat.com

Services

Australasian Spa Association
PO Box 5009, Nowra DC
NSW 2541 Australia
Tel: + 61 2 4422 2206
Fax: + 61 2 4422 3878
Email: aspa@welldone.com.au
www.australasianspaassociation.
com

SpaEscapes.com
*The web gateway to the spas of
Australia and New Zealand*
PO Box 174, Clifton Hill VIC
Australia 3068
Tel: + 61 3 9484 9973
Email: kirien@spaescapes.com
www.spaescapes.com

Spa Guru Consulting
*Consulting to spas in development,
the spa industry, and media on all
things spa*
PO Box 174, Clifton Hill VIC
Australia 3068
Tel: + 61 3 9484 9973
Email: kirien@spaguru.com.au
www.spaguru.com.au

Spa Australasia Magazine
*For spa developers and
spa professionals*
PO Box 55, Glebe NSW
Australia 2037
Subscriptions: Tel: + 61 2 9660 2113
Email: fran@intermedia.com.au
Editorial & Advertising:
Tel: + 61 3 9484 9973
Email: kirien@spaguru.com.au

State Tourism
Agencies

Tourism NSW
Tel: 13 2077 (within Australia)
www.visitnsw.com.au

Tourism Victoria
Tel: 13 2842 (within Australia)
www.visitvictoria.com

Queensland Holiday Xperts
Tel: 1300 730 039 (within Australia)
www.qhx.com.au

Tourism Australia
Tel: + 61 2 9360 1111
www.australia.com

Products

Air Spa
PO Box 1302, Byron Bay NSW 2481
Tel: + 61 2 9560 0568
Fax: + 61 2 9560 0568
www.airspa.com

Australian Bush Flower Essences
45 Booralie Road
Terrey Hills NSW 2084
Tel: + 61 2 9450 1388
Fax: + 61 2 9450 2866
Email: info@ausflowers.com.au
www.ausflowers.com.au

Li'Tya
*Spa care from the Australian
dreamtime*
19 Venture Way
Braeside 3195 VIC
Tel: + 61 3 9587 7088
Fax: + 61 3 9587 7058
Email: admin@litya.com
www.litya.com

In Essence Aromatherapy
221 Kerr Street, Fitzroy
Melbourne 3065 VIC
Tel: + 61 3 9486 9688
Fax: + 61 3 9486 9388
www.inessence.com.au

MV Organics Skincare
PO Box 391, Cammeray NSW 2062
Tel: + 61 2 9909 8315
Email: info@mvskincare.com.au
www.mvskincare.com.au

OP Therapy
19-25 Nelson Road, Yennora
NSW 2161
Tel: + 61 2 9632 0441
Fax: + 61 2 9632 9099
www.optherapy.com.au

Purity Australia
221 Kerr Street, Fitzroy VIC 3065
Tel: + 61 3 8412 9600
www.purityaustralia.com

Sodashi
126 Stirling Highway, North Fremantle
Western Australia 6159
Tel: + 61 8 9336 6837
Fax: + 61 8 9336 7754
www.sodashi.com